AF078570

No Lost Causes Club

No Lost Causes Club

An Honest Guide to Recovery,
and How to Find Your
Way Through It

Lauren McQuistin

4th ESTATE • London

4th Estate
An imprint of HarperCollins*Publishers* Ltd
1 London Bridge Street
London SE1 9GF

www.4thestate.co.uk

HarperCollins*Publishers*
Macken House, 39/40 Mayor Street Upper
Dublin 1, D01 C9W8, Ireland

First published in Great Britain in 2025 by 4th Estate

1

Copyright © Lauren McQuistin 2025

Lauren McQuistin asserts the moral right to be identified
as the author of this work in accordance with the
Copyright, Designs and Patents Act 1988

A catalogue record for this book is
available from the British Library

ISBN 978-0-00-868516-4 (hardback)

All rights reserved. No part of this publication may be reproduced,
stored in a retrieval system, or transmitted, in any form or by any means,
electronic, mechanical, photocopying, recording or otherwise,
without the prior written permission of the publishers.

Without limiting the author's and publisher's exclusive rights, any unauthorised
use of this publication to train generative artificial intelligence (AI) technologies is
expressly prohibited. HarperCollins also exercise their rights under Article 4(3) of the
Digital Single Market Directive 2019/790 and expressly reserve this publication from
the text and data mining exception.

This book is sold subject to the condition that it shall not, by
way of trade or otherwise, be lent, re-sold, hired out or otherwise
circulated without the publisher's prior consent in any form of
binding or cover other than that in which it is published and
without a similar condition including this condition being
imposed on the subsequent purchaser.

Set in Bell MT Std by HarperCollins*Publishers* India

Printed and bound in the UK using 100% Renewable
Electricity at CPI Group (UK) Ltd

This book contains FSC™ certified paper and other controlled
sources to ensure responsible forest management.

For more information visit: www.harpercollins.co.uk/green

For Nicholas

This book is an honest account of addiction, severe mental distress and my path out of that place. Whilst my aim is for it to be a guide to aid you on a recovery journey, it isn't a replacement for professional help, a treatment plan or peer support – things many of us may need (as you will find out if you keep reading, I certainly did).

If you are experiencing mental health difficulties or suicidal ideation, please seek the appropriate professional help. Below are some resources which may also be helpful.

Mind - 0300 123 3393
The Samaritans - 116 123
Calm - 0800 58 58 58
Shout - Text: 85258
Drinkline - 0300 123 1110
Drinkline Scotland - 0800 7314 314
Alcoholics Anonymous - 0800 9177650
Narcotics Anonymous - 0300 999 1212
Al-Anon - 0800 0086 811
SMART Recovery - https://smartrecovery.org.uk/
Recovery Dharma - https://www.recoverydharma.co.uk/

Contents

Introduction		1
Part I		15
I.	Rock Bottom	17
II.	Fear	32
III.	Early Days	50
Part II		69
IV.	Senses	71
V.	Emotions	85
VI.	Escapism	107
Part III		131
VII.	Getting into the World	133
VIII.	The Internet	157
IX.	When Things Get Hard	182
Part IV		201
X.	Sex and Love	203
XI.	Dating	224

Part V 243
    XII. Regret 245
    XIII. Repair and Restoration 260

Conclusion 279
Acknowledgements 287
Endnotes 289

Introduction

When I was 25, I felt like my options were to get sober or kill myself – not a place I thought I would reach when I started drinking as a teenager, feeling like I'd cracked the code to the universe with this *thing* that made me funnier, braver and more comfortable in my skin.

I was 13 when I got drunk for the first time, at the 2006 Battle of the Bands in Stranraer, my remote hometown on the West Coast of Scotland, known mostly for a ferry port to Ireland that is no longer there. The boy I liked was buying me a Blue WKD. I sat on his knee, kissing him with my sweet, blue mouth, dreaming of a bigger future for myself as amateur covers played in the background. I took my first drug around the same time. When I asked what it was, the friend who gave it to me said, with a smirk, that it was an antidepressant. It wasn't, but I certainly didn't feel depressed after I'd taken it. It was freedom; it made me forget the fear, the insecurity and the parts of myself that I hated. I could elevate pleasure, I could diminish pain, I could feel nothing. Alcohol and drugs answered every prayer. It was fun until it wasn't, and they worked until they didn't.

This isn't a story unique to me. Leslie Jamison describes in her memoir *The Recovering: Intoxication and Its Aftermath* (2018), 'Addiction is always a story that has already been told, because it inevitably repeats itself, because it grinds down — ultimately, for everyone — to the same demolished reductive and recycled core: Desire. Use. Repeat.'

When you drink to escape a dark, scared thing inside of you, it can grow teeth the more you ignore it. The more it gnaws at you, the more your self-soothing becomes self-destruction. Your methods of hiding from pain become a new source of it — but by then you're stuck, perhaps thinking those methods will magically start working again.

We all have our reasons why we started drinking. What I didn't realise was that after you experience a physical, interpersonal or psychological consequence as a result of drinking, continuing to drink exactly as you did before, allowing the same dangerous and tragic things to happen, means you may not have a safe relationship with alcohol. For people who are able to have alcohol as a safe part of their life, there is little struggle in choosing not to drink, or managing a single negative emotion without blasting themselves into the sun with a night of face-numbing destruction. Almost everyone with a human liver has felt the effects of a heavy night out; usually it will make them slow down or adjust their choices. If you don't have a safe relationship with alcohol, it isn't that simple. We all have our reasons why stopping can be harder than we ever imagined.

It's hard to explain to someone who hasn't experienced it what it's like not to be able to stop drinking once you start; to have enough willpower to do anything you set your mind to, apart from putting down a substance you are physically or emotionally addicted to. I started drinking, kept drinking when

I shouldn't have, and couldn't stop drinking even when I wanted to because it all felt so painful, awkward and excruciating to be a human. It might have started out as fun, but it became a survival mechanism. My pain didn't travel easily with me; it tore through me and spilled out the edges through self-injury, eating disorders, self-sabotage and public meltdowns. At times, drinking was the least destructive and most socially acceptable thing I could have done to manage the pain, until it became the thing that was making everything worse, and people told me I should think about getting sober.

Not only did sobriety seem impossible, I didn't see the point. People told me I was young and it would give me a chance at life, but the word 'young' didn't mean much to me unless I was using it as an excuse to make poor life choices. I had never felt young; I grew up fast, was aged by trauma and haggard by self-loathing. I didn't feel full of potential; I was an exhausted, depressed, freelance renter who just wanted to feel OK at any cost (but not by getting sober; that would be preposterous). I was young, feeling like I hadn't had a chance to thrive yet, but also that I'd peaked and burnt out too soon.

I thought sobriety was for people who needed to get their life back on track, and I'd never actually been on it. I'd never been in a position to get enough to lose in the first place. My demons never got me to create great music or art. I wasn't on the edge of throwing away a career-making opportunity. I'd never even developed a stable sense of self, or ever felt like I belonged here. What's more, the world was fucked; I couldn't understand why we weren't all drinking in the morning to deal with it.

I wasn't getting sober to save a marriage; I wasn't married. I wasn't getting sober to get my mortgage payments on track; I'd never bought a house. I wasn't getting sober to save my job; my career had barely started. I wasn't getting sober for my health; I couldn't get the time off work for a doctor's appointment. I wasn't getting sober for a family or fertility issues; I didn't have any kids and now, fuck, I'd have to decide if I wanted kids or not. How could I consider being a mother if I couldn't take the dirty dishes out of my bedroom and put them in the sink?

I felt like a failed experiment of a human adult, a complete lost cause. Regardless of what I had or hadn't lost, I felt like a stray, in a world I didn't understand and didn't want to be a part of.

But I wasn't alone. No one my age grew up in the world our parents grew up in. None of us neatly fitted in to their mainstream formula of success. As a young person I lived through two recessions, and I didn't know anyone who had successfully gone to university, landed a job, bought a house, had 2.5 kids and took foreign holidays with them every year. Not all of us had a head start at reaching society's expectations of us, and the gaps were getting bigger. Most of us were struggling to find lasting and meaningful connections as society grew faster, more immediate and more distant. We needed a full-time job, a side-hustle, two degrees and four years of experience for a salary that barely covered the rent of a flat-share, as the threat of a global financial crisis loomed over us. So many of us felt disposable and replaceable in the dating field, workplace and rental market, and we had to work out what self-care (or even just self-preservation) looked like under late-stage capitalism.

We'd witnessed the genesis of the internet, had easy and constant access to more information than anyone could conceive of and stood at the dawn of the AI revolution. We watched daily videos of atrocities – a world in perma-crisis that was only getting worse, and politicians didn't listen or care. We read news about the ocean literally being on fire as people became climate refugees, and were then instructed to manage our carbon footprint as cruelty, greed, propaganda and sponsored content ruled the world.

None of us could afford anything; we were all exhausted – and told we needed to grow up, work harder, smarter and better, then we would achieve the same success as generations before. We should probably start investing; if we haven't, we'll be fucked by the time we retire. If we haven't been wearing SPF 50 since we were 19, we won't be fuckable by the time we're 40 unless we started preventative Botox three years ago, but it's OK, we can talk about our mental-health issues now – as long as they fit into a narrow category of socially acceptable problems, are surmounted in six weeks, don't make us unproductive and don't make anyone uncomfortable.

Why would I want to get sober for that? How could anyone be present for this?

But here's what I realised: there is an unbreakable, rebellious, tenacious and persistent little something inside me, and I believe inside all of us. It was the thing that raged against injustices, the 'no' when things were unfair. It was what wanted to question contradictions and challenge the way things were, and it was the thing that wanted change. It got beaten down with hopelessness, quietened by fear, and came out the edges as hedonism or nihilism – but when I listened to it and realised it was telling me something important, it became the thing that wanted me to get better, rather than be taken under.

Sometimes connecting with this part of myself is painful; it can feel like too much to bear in a world that seems cynical, callous and productivity measured. But this thing knows that I don't have to follow a path that doesn't exist any more, and blatantly wasn't working. This thing inside me believed I could make a new one. It realises I don't have to live up to anyone else's ideas, and that change is possible.

It was the buried-deep desire to live, not just keep buying things and numbing myself out. I wanted to live a life where I wasn't in pain any more, rather than just shoving the pain down with substances and behaviours. The first step in this process was my choice to get sober, to finally confront and address the painful thing. From that place, of agency and choice, I could see what would happen if I stepped out of the ring of falling apart because I felt like I was falling short of what I thought the world expected of me. Everyone else around me might have still been having fun with alcohol and drugs, but at 25 years old, my journey with it was done. I was starting a new one.

My formal training is in opera – an unconventional choice for the daughter of eighth-generation tenant farmers. Hearing it on the radio, I didn't understand the languages, nor did I have any awareness of the class barriers and elitism that would make my future in it extremely difficult – I just heard people feeling things and screaming unreservedly in agony or rapture about it. I had never related to anything more in my entire life. I was always drawn to the 'mad scene', where someone sings a ten-minute aria as they descend into insanity. Usually, it's after they've been raped, society collapses or some terrible injustice has occurred – considering that, you can understand why they would lose their mind. It isn't because they're weak or stupid; they're reacting directly to the horrors of their reality. I don't want to romanticise my mental illness by relating it to an art form – it's hard to do so after being in an NHS psych-ward – but I will say I was a highly sensitive person, feeling the weight of the world upon me and reacting in the only way I knew how, without any tools to deal with it. My 'madness' burst through and got my attention – something needed to change. What if we stopped calling the soprano 'mad', gave her the help she needed and things got better?

What do I mean when I say recovery?

This book is a guide for the challenges that arise throughout the stages of a recovery journey. It will discuss what to expect when we get sober, and strategies to get the most out of it and put it towards the purpose of a life worth living. It will explore everything from making the decision to change and the fears therein, to managing the early days, navigating our mental health, connecting with ourselves, mapping our emotions, recognising escapism behaviours and re-integrating into the world, as well as friendships, loss, dating, sex, regret, growing up, moving on and all the things we don't always talk about when we talk about recovery. I will share my own story and experiences, unpack and expand on each subject, offer the testimonies of my friends, and finish each section with the wisdom and experience I have picked up along the way.

I write through the lens of 'getting sober', as my personal journey is one of abstinence, but I'm always speaking just as much to those who are aiming for a different destination or haven't decided exactly where they want to end up yet. Getting untangled from the life we want out of can mean many different things to many different people – this book can be used as a framework for simply getting to a different place, or working out exactly what that place looks like for you. Abstinence is a practice of not engaging with mind-altering substances, and sobriety involves the process of learning how to react proportionally to life, living in line with your values and acting in a way that is beneficial for your most authentic self and those around you. Recovery is returning to, or finding, a state of wholeness and restoring what was lost, which for me requires abstinence.

This book is for absolutely anyone who wants to explore what change might look like for them. I cannot tell you how to get sober, I can simply share my experience, and outline the avenues available. There are many paths to recovery, as there are many ways to change – you can explore if you need a framework such as the twelve-step programme or other mutual help groups, if you wish to be supported by therapy or medications, and if you need to abstain from all mind-altering substances, your primary drug of choice or a behaviour. To determine what you need requires honesty with yourself, and a willingness to truly investigate the nature of what you're dealing with.

There is no path to growth I want to promote or discredit. The only right way to recover is the one that works for you.

Here's the thing, getting sober is hard

I used to think that if I could just stop drinking, doing drugs, seeking the validation of strange men, bingeing, purging and running sharp objects along my skin, I'd be sorted. Not doing those things mitigated some damage – but without them I was left with the pain I was using them to avoid, and that pain led me back to the destructive behaviour. Things fall apart; the centre cannot hold; your life becomes a never-ending cycle of the same story.

When you start taking the antidepressants, get into eating-disorder recovery, begin trauma therapy or stop drinking, there's a temptation to believe that's you sorted now. You can start being *normal* now. But really, you've only just taken the first step towards an ongoing process – and sometimes the process can be painful, and gets worse before it gets better.

People don't want to see unhappy sober people, they want to see people putting the drink down and doing well – because that's the story that makes us feel better about the fact that mental-health issues and addiction are life-ruining, lethal, confusing conditions that destroy lives, families and generations. So it makes sense that when we talk about the struggle of sobriety we talk about the struggle of getting sober, rather than the reality that staying stopped can sometimes be just as hard as stopping. We can focus overwhelmingly on the positives of sobriety, for fear of what the alternative option looks like.

Change happens once we stop struggling in silence with our pain, so we cannot struggle in silence in our recovery. This book will discuss the struggles of not just getting sober, but of sobriety as a whole, and how to struggle well, with honesty and hope.

Recovery is hard, not just because you don't know what to do with your hands at parties, but because in the early days you're terrified, bewildered, irritable, horny and grieving something you don't want back. You're learning how to live without your only familiar method of dealing with life. Everything becomes a new frontier again. You lose the horizon and are looking for those things that can only be found in the wild, which can sometimes make you feel like an absolute failure. Sobriety is difficult because being a human is difficult, especially when you haven't got a lot of experience of existing without substances that make you forget the very fact that you are a human.

Sobriety isn't as simple as 'before' and 'after'. It's a practice. It's putting something down and seeing what you're dealing with. It's finding what works and what doesn't, trying again and trying something different, to build a life you don't want to run away from, over time and with continued effort. I had to break the rigid thinking of the world being full of 'fucked-up, drunk good-for-nothings' and 'perfect sober individuals who do everything right and have flawless skin'. It didn't work having the only two options as 'failure' or 'success story'. Working out how to be human is ongoing and never-ending, and it reaches no conclusions – so it's probably a good idea to start enjoying it, which might involve trying something different. What gave me the courage to try was not imagining sobriety as a destination or achievement. It was something I was willing to try as part of a process, to turn a dragged-out, miserable existence into part of a larger story.

A note on language

I identify as an alcoholic or addict; it is just one of the many things that I am: a musician, a member of many communities, a Scottish woman, an Aquarius, a writer and a person in recovery. This label is not to keep myself stuck in my past or limit myself; it is a neutral acknowledgement of something I deal with, so I can keep seeking the help I need and grow. It is not to blame or shame myself, because I do not believe addicts or alcoholics are bad people; they are, in fact, the people I love the most in the entire world. Many people prefer to use person-first or identity-first language, some call it substance-use disorder, while others feel no need to name it. However we identify, whatever opinions or reactions we have on or to the language of recovery, the point we can agree on is that we use whatever terms we use because they are helpful to us, and it is a personal choice.

Throughout this book I will use the word addiction, but I don't believe people have to consider themselves addicts to have experienced addiction or want to change. Addiction physician and bioethicist Carl Erik Fisher discusses in *The Urge: Our History of Addiction* (2022) how addiction is deeply human:

> Addiction is profoundly ordinary: a way of being with the pleasures and pains of life, and just one manifestation of the central human task of working with suffering. If addiction is part of humanity, then, it is not a problem to solve. We will not end addiction, but we must find ways of working with it: ways that are sometimes gentle, and sometimes vigorous, but never warlike, because it is futile to wage war on our own nature.

Sobriety doesn't have an age bracket

Data compiled by UK charity Drinkaware shows that in 2019 16- to 25-year-olds were the most likely to be teetotal, with 26 per cent not drinking.[1] A study at the University of Michigan from 2020 found that the portion of college-age Americans who are teetotal has risen from 20 per cent to 28 per cent in a decade.² Gen Z and Millennials are more impacted by financial and societal worries, and because we are seeing what isn't working, we are more likely to ask ourselves questions about how we want to live and what isn't serving us. We talk about our mental health in ways that haven't been acceptable before. We know more about the risks, we have the platforms to tell our story and we discuss it openly, often defiantly.

While more people than ever are not drinking, it doesn't make sobriety easier for people who have it as a difficult choice, or those who put the drink down and don't know what to do now. Gen Z might be more sober, but they are not happier. According to Cigna International Health's 2023 survey, 91 per cent of 18 to 24-year-olds report being stressed – compared to the 84 per cent average across all age ranges.³ Young people are drinking less, however the Scottish Public Health Survey found in 2019 that dependant drinking is more common among younger people, with those between 16 and 24 being more than twice as likely to exhibit drinking patterns suggestive of alcohol dependence than any other age category,⁴ and according to youth charity The Mix, there has been a 75 per cent increase since 2021 in young people using drugs.⁵

We have access to therapy, content and language that give us our more personal insight and reflection than any generation. So many of us are realising that we were neurodivergent all along, and have been overcompensating our whole lives to survive in a world that wasn't designed for us. This knowledge about ourselves is an important place to start – now we get to think: *What now? What am I going to do with this information?*

Getting sober is a personal choice, and something bigger than us. It plugs us into a world where we can choose where we put our energy and effort, where we can practise self-care to take better care of each other. Sobriety isn't just a change in one behaviour: it's changing your actions, thoughts and beliefs about yourself and the world. It changes your entire life, and the lives of those around you.

Things like compassionate care and trauma-informed treatment are becoming more common and are in greater demand, because our bodies have been keeping the score for too long (see page 78). We're at an important time in history where we realise that our issues can't be ignored, shamed or belittled away. While these behaviours we are stuck in are hard to understand, we have everything a human has, and we deserve compassion, dignity and help. This is the No Lost Causes Club, and I am so glad we are all here.

PART I

Nothing changes if nothing changes – how to make a start.

I. Rock Bottom

It is in the knowledge of the genuine conditions of our life that we must draw our strength to live and our reason for acting.

— Simone de Beauvoir,
The Ethics of Ambiguity (1947)

When you can no longer keep saying, 'I'm handling it,' as your life falls apart but don't know what else to do. When you get trapped in the place of knowing you need to change, but you don't feel like it's bad enough yet. When the thing that you were always sure would make you feel better has stopped working, but you're not sure you can let it go.

Overture: A party scene where the soprano realises she doesn't drink like everyone else

It's early 2018 and I'm somewhere before Act Two, Scene Two, on stage at the Shubert Theatre in New Haven, climbing on top of a long table and singing a quintet in German. I'm styled as a malfunctioning robot in this production of *The Magic Flute*, wearing a dress the shape of a purple triangle, a cherry-red wig and platform shoes that leave a trail of glitter behind them. I'm being yelled at over the orchestra because I'm not watching the conductor and it's throwing off the ensemble. I ignore it; I have to focus on not falling off this fucking table.

A couple of days earlier, after a chaotic rehearsal of doing my best badly, the director had told me to get it right or get out. Up to this point I'd been telling myself that drinking during the rehearsal period helped me quieten my inner critic and take more dramatic risks. But the risks of this artistic process were becoming less about fully embodying a character, and more about my failing academic transcript, disappearing for days after jumping into cars with strangers and losing what was left of my sanity.

Everyone who knew me knew that I *drank*. I would be the first to suggest another round when everyone else was only a quarter of the way through the current one. I would show up at your house with two bottles of wine and finish both of them myself. I was always willing, always available for a night of debauchery and poor judgement. I was the libertine, a bohemian; I would be having a good time whatever the cost. I thought everyone was white-knuckling to the point where we could legitimately have a drink, and I was just renegade enough to live truthfully, brave enough to rebel against the notions of what was 'appropriate'. I thought everyone's thoughts were consumed by alcohol when they weren't drinking, and that we were all in the dance of justifying drinking more than we should at times when we shouldn't, because if it's customary to have a drink in the airport bar before a flight, then surely you could be blackout for a yoga class or a five-year-old's birthday party?

It was easy to believe when I started music school in Glasgow in 2011, when everyone was discovering the world around them with cheap shots and bad decisions, but when people started leaving the pub early for rehearsal the next day or could say no to a night out, I realised that not everyone was drinking like I was. What's more, I was becoming a bit too miserable for someone who described themselves as a hedonist.

I knew I was depressed, but we were all depressed, we were all traumatised (we were in music school, after all). We all had our assorted experiences of life becoming unfair, we all had hungry hearts with a need to feel seen and a drive for perfection that made us want to be musicians in the first place. Drinking was my way of dealing with it; it gave me a thrill of temporary relief. But the relief period started to grow shorter. When it eventually disappeared, I didn't know what else to do other than hope it came back. I thought as time went on it would sort itself out. I would calm down; something would shift inside me; drinking would become the solution again. I thought if I kept pretending it was working it eventually would. I thought that if I kept convincing people it was my choice, then I would believe it.

I tried to moderate but would just watch everyone's drinks, wondering how a human being could drink so slowly. No matter how the night started, how many timers I set telling me to switch to water, or how many people I told to slap the glass out of my hand if they saw me drinking past 10 p.m., I always ended up in the same place. By my second year of university, not even 20 yet, I knew drinking wasn't about elevating pleasure any more, it was about diminishing pain. It felt like literally the only thing I could do to make me feel OK about, well, everything.

Act One, Scene One: Flashback, a sheep farm on the West Coast of Scotland

I, like many Scottish people, started drinking young, because what else was there to do in a diminishing ferry town in the country once hailed as the 'drug-death capital of Europe'? Drinking wasn't simply something to alleviate boredom, it was my passport to acting like a 'normal' person. Drinking loosened the aching, self-conscious knot inside me; my thoughts went more slowly – I thought this must be how other people felt all the time. I was someone who people said 'felt things very deeply'. When I found out that the oceans were being polluted I was inconsolable, and the blows kept coming: I discovered the situation in the rainforests, the fact that plastic bags take 100 years to decompose, and the painful realities of sickness and death. The more I learned about the world, the more I feared it, but I also felt a responsibility to fix it and a deep hopelessness that I couldn't. When school progressed and cliques formed, I was the designated weirdo, then a target of bullying and ostracisation. It started a battle between wanting to be loved and accepted for who I was, but also wanting to keep everyone as far away from me as possible, so that I would never be hurt or rejected again.

When you grow up wondering where your home planet is because it can't be *here*, you're told that you'll find your friends as time goes on, you'll find where you belong, it gets easier. You flick down to 'early life' on every celebrity's Wikipedia page, hoping that they, too, were from a small town or grew up feeling like an outsider before they found their way to global fame, where they were seen and accepted. You journal about what life might be like when things are different, when that voice inside that tells you you're a stupid piece of shit stops dominating your opinion of yourself. Whether this would all come true or not, this hopeful future can seem too far from the unbearable present.

I couldn't save the oceans or the rainforests, and I would never fit in here – but I could drink and do drugs.

By 21, I was starting to feel less like I was a spiralling woman in an eight-episode Netflix series about how the fun and quirky gal pulls it all back together, and more like I was trapped in a routine of hating myself for the things I did when I was drinking and then drinking to deal with the shame of that. I was so busy punishing and despising myself for not reacting normally to life that I couldn't even come up with devastating and hilarious lines for the camera any more. The toll on my body couldn't be taken away by a glass of water and a piece of toast. People were distancing themselves from me, because the libertine was becoming a liability. Things we used to scream-laugh about over the kitchen table with hangovers and Sports Direct mugs full of instant coffee just weren't funny any more. Not everyone was getting hospitalised after a night out, having arguments over whether they were flirting with someone's boyfriend or not, or embarrassing themselves at industry events. People didn't want to be around someone who just talked about themselves, their drama and their hangover all the time. The fact that I 'just didn't have an off switch' wasn't an eccentric characteristic any more. I realised that the time-travelling and teleportation of blackouts were a shocking exception for other people, rather than an inevitability. But I'd got really good at damage control, I was handling it – this was how people like me handled it. When I graduated in 2015 I decided Scotland was the problem and moved to the USA to do a master's degree at Indiana University. I got a scholarship for it, and triumphantly thought to myself, See. *It isn't* that *bad*.

Act One, Scene Two: I thought the soprano was supposed to die at the end – she already isn't looking too good

So now I was 25, doing another master's degree, this time at Yale University, in my first assignment as Erste Dame in *The Magic Flute*. I made it off the table without falling, but the conductor was shaking his head in disappointment. I had missed my solo-line entrance as my voice spun in another orbit, away from the centreless pit of my body. I was trying to hit my next mark, to embrace my stage partner, when the dizziness took me over. I ran off-stage, my little glitter path behind me, and was violently sick. I didn't stop to see if people were looking, I didn't know if the orchestra had stopped – I just ran.

My stage make-up melted under the dressing-room lights as I started to cry, trying to rub the smears of foundation and eyeshadow off my hands. I couldn't breathe – a vice-like grip moved from the bottom of my lungs to my throat, choking me. I made a nest of jackets and lay in the corner of the room, still in costume, shaking. Some nurturing voice inside said, 'Try to sleep, try to breathe.' A voice from an inky-black hollow said, 'Your mother will have a dead daughter.' The jaded, exhausted part of myself, a bitchy former It-girl, smoking a cigarette by a French window thinking this was all a bit pathetic, said, 'Why today? It's tech week.' God, I wanted a drink.

Curled up on the dressing-room floor, I remembered a morning just before I moved to the US, waking up on a wet mattress, trying to convince my friend that I was just a sweaty sleeper. We worked part-time in a department store together and were renowned for being agents of chaos. We would trade prescription pills in the jewellery-counter giftboxes, laugh at the inane absurdity of life quoting *All About Eve*, and organise nights out that ended with drug-fuelled scenarios like a floor manager panicking on my living-room floor thinking he'd gone blind because someone put a sheet over his head. He, supposedly my ally in mayhem, turned to me and said: 'I'm scared for you.'

He slept next to me, because he was scared that I would roll onto my back and choke on my vomit. As I downed the warm glass of water he had left on my bedside table, I told him that it was fine, it would never get that bad again. Until it did a few days later when I had to beg him to cover for me at work for being late, and help me tidy my flat before my boyfriend came over, after a busy night of cheating and doing drugs with strangers in my living room.

I didn't want to stop drinking, I just wanted to stop the consequences. I just wanted to have fun, make people laugh, feel like I was part of something and not care how I looked; I just needed to work out how to drink without blacking out.

I still hadn't worked it out, all these years later, 3,218 miles away from what I thought was a problem. In the process pain had become my baseline, and fleeting but recurring embarrassment turned into deep, calcified shame. I promised myself I would never perform drunk in the USA, until I found myself in a production of *Peter Grimes*, on the edge of a blackout in front of an audience of 1,000 people. That night I wrote, 'I wish I was sober, I wish I was sober, I wish I was sober,' in my journal. For a week I hid from my inbox, for fear of a 'we know what you did' email. No one said anything, and I realised I'd got away with it. So I did it again, hating myself for the fact that I couldn't stay sober for the thing I loved the most in the world and was unable to keep a promise to myself to protect something I'd defeated the odds to achieve.

Off-stage, my safety and dignity were repeatedly violated, but I edited the things that happened to me in post – waking up, confused and sore, in a stranger's bed became a salacious anecdote. Then I would drink to forget, and walk home alone in an unknown neighbourhood with a dead phone. I rationalised drinking alone as a self-care ritual. When I returned home after a long day of hanging on by a fucking thread, hearing the click of the door-latch was the safe assurance that I could do what I liked now, no one was watching. Here I was a creative genius, a tragic image of romanticised suffering, accessing the darkness that few could understand. Misanthropy and suspicion of other people felt like a normal, almost healthy mistrust that put me in the league of great thinkers, writers and artists that society loves now that they have been recast as icons and pioneers of their time, before the monsters in their head won. I insisted I needed a direct line to my demons to make music, act and write, though I hadn't read a book in years because my mental health was an abyss. The more I numbed myself with this cycle, the more I detached myself from my experiences, as if they were happening to someone else. If I stayed there, the consequences didn't matter. I crossed the invisible line of 'you'd be better off dead' and started to think it wouldn't be so bad if I didn't wake up in the morning. It was my escape hatch – a cold comfort when my head hit the pillow.

Act One, Scene Three: I don't know if we're going to get an Act Two

On the dressing-room floor I saw someone's face between the blur of my eyelids, and I went from the dressing room to the New Haven Health Centre to speak with a doctor. I sat in the waiting room, not wanting to tell my friends what had happened, because it would mean acknowledging I had a problem – that no matter how far and fast I ran I couldn't escape myself. I couldn't remember the last time I had talked to my family, simply because I didn't want them to find out what a disappointment I was. I was alone, just me and the vicious voice in my head. I was tired. It had been a long day.

I walked into an office with 'Peace' and 'Breathe' canvases in sloping letters next to stiff prescription manuals and a ticking clock. I couldn't look anyone in the eye, and my breath had still not returned to my body. *I could just kill myself,* I thought, *or move to a different country again.*

The doctor put my file gently on the small wooden table beside her and said, 'We're going to get you help.'

A voice inside me, one I had never listened to before, said calmly, 'Please take the help.' It came from somewhere small and still, an uncharted place. It was a long-forgotten part of me that wanted to live. The clock ticked. The chaos raging in my skull separated, and in that cyclone's eye it said: 'You're done.'

When this voice was a whisper, I laughed it off, saying, 'I'm young, fun and not doing anything anyone else isn't doing.' I ignored it in quiet moments when my headphones died and I was faced with the diabolical landscape of my internal monologue, telling me something needed to change. It would scream at me during hangovers as I was gripping the edges of my mattress to stop the room from tipping over. I'd heard it but never really listened. I'd been here before, and every time I told myself it wasn't that bad.

It could get worse. But this voice was telling me now maybe time was up.

Before my head had the chance to tell me, *It's fine, you're fine, you're handling it*, I looked at the doctor and heard myself say, 'OK.'

For some of us, the party ends earlier than we expected. It might have started as a night to remember, but there's a moment when we realise it isn't living up to what we wanted it to be. The lights come on, and we're faced with the reality outside of the mythology. We catch our reflection in a mirror and think, *Oh, God, I'm fucked.*

Your rock bottom doesn't have to be the worst things can get. It's the moment you don't want it to get any worse

When you are confronted with the reality of your drinking, it can be tempting to compile a list of things that render you 'not bad enough' to warrant change, especially when, despite what it's taking, drinking can feel like something that's holding you together. It's impossible to picture a world without it; you don't know how to socialise, date, enjoy yourself or even go to the post office without it, even though it's starting to take more than it's giving, and aggressively smoking a cigarette out of the window pretending it isn't happening won't fix it.

You might maintain the outward appearance of someone who is holding it together, but waking up in the morning carries a dark dread of knowing that you're alive. This can be harder to move out of than a catastrophic, life-ruining event; it's harder to notice and easier to hide. When there's some semblance of functionality, you can defend alcohol's position in your life, even though the bar is slowly getting lower and you're gradually accepting the unacceptable more. The more you descend, the harder it is to get out. You close the curtains, open your laptop and wish you didn't exist any more, getting ready to do it all over again.

You can make the case for it not being that bad, such as not having custody battles, jails or rehabs in your story. You have some friends left, you've only missed rent once or twice, you can speak foreign languages and know how to bake a cake from scratch, therapists find you funny, you're really good at winged eyeliner, you have candles, crystals and all the self-help books. I would think, *I'm not even anyone's ex-wife yet. Surely it should take longer to completely destroy your life.*

You can meet your rock bottom and move in. The more you trundle along the bottom of barely hanging on, the more you accept that you're built to live below the misery line. Promises you make to yourself to change something start to crumble more easily the more practice you have at giving up on them. Even if things get darker and deeper, you begin to put up less of a fight and decide to just live with it. You find yourself saying, 'Well, I knew this was going to happen anyway.' The more you ignore the inner voice telling you that you can't keep doing this, the more you diminish and slice off parts of your soul piece by piece.

What you're left with is the grim reality that whether the consequences are physical, emotional, mental, spiritual or psychological, they lead you to a place where you need to take something out of the equation, or continue the damage-control mission until something happens that you can't talk, scheme or bargain your way out of.

Rock bottom can be destitution, homelessness or families reading letters to you about how your drinking is affecting them –

but it can also just be the thing that finally gets your attention, and gives you the desire to change, whether that's an event or an unignorable feeling. It can be the strangely hopeful thought of, *I don't want to feel like this any more*, when you realise that trying to maintain that you're the poster girl of fun (crying in the bathroom, looking in the mirror and telling yourself, 'This is fun, I am having a *good* time') is coming at too high a cost. Realistically, no matter what it looks like on the outside, no matter how old you are, if your life feels unbearable, it's bad enough.

Make them laugh, make them cry

When drinking feels like the only pain management for trauma, adverse childhood experiences or the feeling that you are bad and wrong down to the cellular level, you can often find it's easier to hide it in plain sight – make yourself a character far from who you actually are and how you are feeling. You can make it seem like you're having a good time, and put on a hell of a show.

My friend and frequent musical collaborator Danny decided to make a change at the same time I did. He met his rock bottom when a scream inside said, 'This isn't funny. Your life is not a joke. I don't want to be funny, I want to be happy.'

Talking about it now, he says, 'It would have been terrible for someone to know how much I was struggling. I didn't want them to have to bear the burden of knowing that, so I made them comfortable by being funny. I'd think, *It's why people want me around, it's the only thing I'm good for*, because without it I was just another high-functioning, depressed, traumatised or mentally ill person who doesn't know what to do.'

Danny describes this performance as 'so much worse than being an out-of-control mess. There is a relief in falling to pieces, because you feel deserving of asking for help. But when you're funny and sardonic, you are being buried alive. I was watching myself do and say things, thinking, *I know that's not me, but I don't remember who I am.*'

Getting sober isn't reserved for a particular category of person

Whether you're lying down feeling the jagged edges of broken parts on a dressing-room floor, under your desk, rotting in bed or on the floor in front of your dishwasher in the morning as your flatmates walk around you making cups of tea, we can connect on the feeling of emptiness. Whether you are the life and soul of any party, a loner who has forgotten how to connect to people or losing yourself by chameleoning further away from who you actually are, we can connect through the loneliness. Whether you are an exhausted party girl, can't engage with the things that used to light you up inside or are stuck in the grooves of a life you don't want to be living any more, we can connect on the feeling that we're going nowhere. Whether you are at the top or bottom of your career, lost or losing it, we all know that feeling of being lost. Whatever the circumstances, we can connect via the desire to change. If whatever made you pick up this book matches the fear, pain, shame, numbness or trapped feelings that led me to the same point, then we have something in common.

At one point the drugs and alcohol served a purpose. Lacking any other tools, they were the ones we were using to help us deal with things we felt we couldn't face any other way, and like any maladaptive coping mechanism, they eventually stop working.

Desiring change is a realisation you can only have for yourself, and usually you only start listening to that returning voice when you cross a threshold to somewhere deeper and darker than you thought you would go. A ground zero; a soul-snap; a point where you are unable to go on as you are, knowing what you now know.

If you have that realisation, act on it. Immediately. Don't wait to address it tomorrow, because the clarity, hope or motivation to do something about it might be eclipsed by the urge or familiarity to keep going in the only way you know how. Write it down, make it tangible, and then back it up with action. Call a helpline, research services in your area or go to a meeting. If services are overloaded or unavailable, tell someone in your circle. Talk to a friend who's sober and ask what they did. Do anything you can while the feeling is with you. Be brave enough to be honest – they might already know (we are less sneaky than we think, and people are more insightful than we give them credit for). Take the help and don't talk yourself out of it when it's offered to you. You can acknowledge that you're frightened – they're used to that.

You can ask yourself what you have to lose by doing something different or trying something difficult. It's a call for compassion for yourself, and recognition that you don't have to sort it all out today – but you can make a start.

There's an old cliché that rock bottom is the point where you stop digging; it can always get deeper. You don't need to wait for some singular event to decide to simply put the shovel down. If you don't want what you have, you can try something different –

it's as simple as that. If you have found yourself googling, 'Am I an alcoholic?' at 3 a.m., or you are in that strange middle place where life with drink is a nightmare and life without it seems too much to bear, or if you just want out, you're not alone.

If you want to make a change, you can actually work on your mental health rather than hiding from it. You can find out that feelings won't kill you. In fact, the more you engage with them, the better you can develop an intimate relationship, not only with the dark parts of yourself, but with joy, excitement and pleasure. You can connect with people in genuine ways after taking the time to get to know yourself. You can process the painful thing you think you'll never be able to let go of. You can find out exactly what you enjoy and do it without missing a single second of it. You can explore how you want to show up in the world and contribute something to it. You can find a stability, in your inner and outer lives, which can have resilience even when it gets tough. You can see what you are capable of when you aren't allowing alcohol to splinter you into fragmented selves.

No one ever picks up a book about sobriety by accident. Whether your interest is due to a personal investment into considering sobriety, or because someone you know has struggled with substances, it is a close-to-the-bone subject. It requires honesty and vulnerability. Getting sober, and getting through this book, will take both, and my heart is with you every page of the way. It is a lot to take in, and there's a lot of processing ahead, but for today you can perhaps accept that the party is over. It might have ended a long time ago. You might be done.

II. Fear

"Do you have this organ here?" Cyrus asked her, pointing at the base of his throat. "A doom organ that just pulses all the time? Pulses dread, every day, obstinately? Like it thinks there's a panther behind the curtain ready to maul you, but there's no panther and it turns out there's no curtain either? That's what I wanted to stop."
– Kaveh Akbar, *Martyr!* (2024)

When you're facing something new, and it looks bigger than you can handle. When you're scared of things changing, and things staying the same. When the way forward is unclear, and no one can convince you it will be OK.

I never said, 'I am hungover,' or, 'I'm on a comedown.' I always said, on those mornings when I was feeling crispy (paranoid, full of shame and paralysed by the dread of flipping my phone over), 'I have the fear.'

When you've been messing with your dopamine, your serotonin doesn't know what it's doing any more, and your sleep hygiene and blood sugars are critically injured, so your body sometimes overshoots on its way down to 'normal' and lands in 'suicidal'. 'It's just the fear,' I'd say. 'It'll pass.'

My biggest fear used to be that I'd betrayed my carefully curated personality during blackout, eventually it became the fear that the light behind my eyes was fading, and there was a darkness inside me that would one day inevitably win. Everything's scary when you're at war with your drinking; something you depended on has turned on you, but you don't trust that life without it will be any better because you have no idea what that life looks like. We're built to be scared of the unknown, so a lot of the time we will choose the familiar hell over the unfamiliar heaven. Inertia, no matter how painful, can feel safer in its certainty.

Many of us drank to escape, to assuage discomfort, anxiety and insecurity – we drank for bravery in the face of our fears. Getting sober challenges us to face what we've been trying to hide from. It exposes the raw nerves of our deepest fears and fundamental beliefs about ourselves. One of the scariest things we can do is challenge a belief that we have fully committed to, but it's also a valuable experience that can teach us things we can't find out any other way.

Fear of inadequacy

As much as I believed that things weren't bad enough and I was fine, if a little bit dramatic, I simultaneously held a firm conviction that I was inherently broken beyond repair. These two barriers to change wrestled with each other, tied together by the underlying fear of my inherent inadequacy – that I wasn't someone worth helping. Convincing myself and others that things 'weren't bad enough' was protective, because if people knew things were bad and getting worse, the belief that there was something bad about *me* might be confirmed.

If you grow up feeling different, you can spend your early years wondering why you didn't get a copy of the handbook. The secret set of rules for human interactions are a mystery. You watch other kids playing and wonder how they're just *doing* that, and you don't know why people are making fun of you for not understanding social conventions, having 'inappropriate' emotional responses or incorrect niche interests. You feel left in the dark, like your existence is subject to ridicule, leaving you unprotected by the pack. It seeds the idea that there's something wrong about you, and you are simply too different to be loved and accepted. It's a terrifying place for a child to be.

From childhood I tried to convince everyone I was worthy of love by trying to be special, different and talented. My fear-based, doom-operated system helped me tear through books, pathologically practise the piano and get perfect grades to appease the oppressive fear that I wasn't good enough. It worked. I did well in school, was in national singing competitions as the youngest competitor and was praised for being a hard worker. Drinking gave me the same relief, and it was easier.

But it only appeased the fear temporarily, it never eradicated it – whether the fears were 'Will there be enough to get me drunk enough?' and 'When are the drugs coming?' or the existential fear of constantly waiting for the other shoe to drop, or being found out as a fraud, a freak, the lonely kid on the edge of the playground wondering why nobody wants to talk to her.

Fear of being vulnerable

When I met with a therapist, during my first year of university in Glasgow in 2011, I had a concussion. The night before, my ex, Connor, who had dumped me on my birthday, had broken into my building to pester me for sex. After twenty minutes of saying 'no' I eventually gave in, because it was the only certain way he would leave. During this transaction I – drunk – fell off him and hit my head on the bedside cabinet.

Regardless, I dutifully went to therapy the next day. I wanted to tell her that I was supposed to be working out what to do with my life but would rather see myself out than stick around for it. I wanted to say that I'd been lying for a really long time about so many things. I wanted to explain that I was broken, and she couldn't help me, but then scream, 'Please help me!' I wanted to say that every day when I walk into the rehearsal room I am swallowing a secret about the man who taught me how to sing and it all feels like some Greek myth because I want to be a singer to make it all worth it, but this is becoming a bit too much to handle and *you* would drink too if you had to deal with that. But I didn't want to get into all that, and I didn't have words for it. Life got busy. I thought I would work it out by myself, and I didn't go back.

With my next therapist, a year later, I played the role of the 'perfect patient' because I wanted her to feel like she was doing a good job, which meant I obviously couldn't tell her about my drinking. Isolating from my own experience by performing the role of a lifetime (throwing in a few zingers when I felt like the session was getting too heavy), I felt even more lost in the arena where I was supposed to be finding myself. But I had the routine of acting like I was taking her suggestions and pretending to integrate the insight down to an art – until I was trying to buy chewing gum in a petrol station one day, and a load-bearing wall in my psyche suddenly collapsed. Then I was swallowing paracetamol, five at a time, writing a note that said:

> *I'm sorry you ever thought I was getting better. I don't know if I was or if it was fake. It's all just so fake. I seriously thought I would make this more poetic. I love you all, I'm sorry. Don't miss me, I'm happier here.*

And still, when they asked me at the hospital why I tried to kill myself, I told them it was all a huge misunderstanding, and I was completely fine. If I was going to actually kill myself, I would have left a *much* better note.

At the beginning of my recovery in 2018, I told my therapist that I just wanted to feel nothing. She said part of the process would be honestly feeling my feelings, and, honestly, I wanted to hit her. I felt like I physically couldn't handle the experience of acknowledging what I had been through – why else would I have gone to such lengths to forget it? But the first and most important frontier of my recovery was getting honest with someone about what was really going on, and letting them help me.

Carrie Fisher said, 'If my life wasn't funny it would just be true, and that is unacceptable.' Talking with therapists like I was on a talk show, packaging my pain as anecdotes or lying, was easier, but it wasn't working. I needed to get uncomfortable, and let my honesty – even the ugly stuff like wanting to hit your therapist – be the way back to myself.

Fear of failure

I was scared change would be beyond me, because I had tried to sort my life out so many times that I had stopped telling people I was trying. I first attempted to get sober when I was 19, and tried about ten times after, each time buckling under the pressure of any excuse to start drinking again, and claiming sobriety just didn't work. I was so embarrassed at my failure to thrive that I resigned myself to being the renaissance woman of fucking up my life, trying to get sober yet again under the guise of a 'health cleanse' or telling people that doing *The Artist's Way** again was enough to fix me, but never quite being willing to give it everything I had. My attempts at sobriety were always cut short because I always started with the preconceived idea that I would eventually fail.

I thought I was protecting myself from disappointment by getting used to the worst and not hoping for better; as we say in Scotland, 'It's the hope that kills you.' If I really tried, and failed, that would be a humiliation I couldn't bear. Really trying something requires a bit of hope through taking an action you don't know the outcome of. That's where you meet fear. That's what kills you. That's what keeps you in the stuck place of knowing you need to change but being too scared to take the next steps.

---

*   Julia Cameron's twelve-week course to recover, access and utilise your creativity, a book which is recommended to you at least every two weeks if you're in a creative field, and is way more useful to do when you're not smashed beyond recognition all the time.

Fear of the unknown

People often ask me if I ever get stage fright. Honestly, the most comfortable I have ever been was on stage, in someone else's clothes, singing someone else's words in a foreign language, telling a story that had already finished, to a melody that was decided for me. I got real-life fright, existing in reality and doing something where the cadence wasn't already written.

Some people say inner work is like peeling an onion, but I don't think we are a static object to get to the bottom of, or a riddle to solve. I see it like a shedding of skin. There's no final centre to be reached, there's just gradually seeing what's really under the depression, anger, hatred, narratives, limiting beliefs and fear in a process that is constantly evolving. The work begins and can continue if you let it, allowing yourself to change with it. There's no known outcome, just an unfolding process, the way forward becoming clearer as you go.

Fear of what other people think

The word 'sober' carried a sense of loss. It was losing my anaesthetic for life, but maybe also my friends, my creativity and my rebellious nature. Under each of these projected losses was a fear. Fear that my friends actually hated me, that I was a fraud or that I would be tepid, boring and dull.

I described myself as a social drinker because drinking seemed to be the only thing that made me sociable. When I thought about living without it I agonised over what people might think of me. Making a choice to no longer engage with coping mechanisms that exist in other people's lives as quite ordinary things can make you feel like the different one, the boring one, the fragile one. Your personal choices, though entirely your own, can feel up for public scrutiny, and, God, you don't want to be the outsider because you know how cold it gets out there.

When you stop doing something that gives you a sense of identity it's hard to know who you'll be and where you'll fit in without it. I was worried about losing the stories of my escapades. Managing to find my way back from a strange man's house in Ayr with a smashed, dead phone, a mysterious bottle of sparkling wine in an IKEA bag, no shoes and yesterday's dress, and still managing to make the 5 p.m. rehearsal, is a way more interesting story than, 'I got a good night's sleep and learned my music.'

If I wasn't the carefully curated sad-girl-wild-child, then who would I be and what would there be to talk about? If you've never fitted in before, it's fun sometimes to be ballistically inappropriate, and have it be somewhat acceptable. When the world you've grown accustomed to seems insane, it's natural that you just want to flout the norms and do something crazy.

Fear of being 'boring'

Becoming 'boring' felt like a threat of sobriety. But, in reality, I was already so bored. Destroying yourself more quickly than the world will, so it feels like it's your choice, gets boring. Looking for something in the same place you couldn't find it before and saying, 'Who are you?' into the mirror gets boring. You know you're fucked when your baseline of pain gets boring. An exhausted loved one saying, 'You don't remember?' when you ask what you did last night stops being a fun dispatch the morning after and gets boring. Asking yourself, 'How did I get here?' – whether it's in a stranger's bed or a thought pattern that leads to the same misery – is boring. A life that is absolutely devoid of true intimacy because you cannot get close to yourself, never mind anyone else, is boring. Denying yourself the full experience of your life gets more boring as time goes on, even if you make it seem like you're really enjoying it. I felt like people would think I was weird for deciding not to drink in a drinking culture – even though engaging with this culture made me cause scenes, let people down or divulge the most demented parts of my psyche at casual after-work drinks. The harsh reality is that other people were starting to find that boring, too. They were either growing up or stuck in the same place, just as bored as I was now the thrill was gone.

Fear of just being fucking alive

> 'At the core of every addiction is an emptiness based in abject fear. The addict dreads and abhors the present moment; she bends feverishly only toward the next time, the moment when her brain, infused with her drug of choice, will briefly experience itself as liberated from the burden of the past and the fear of the future – the two elements that make the present intolerable.'
> – Gabor Maté, *In the Realm of Hungry Ghosts: Close Encounters with Addiction* (2008)

This emptiness is not only present in people who drink breakfast vodka. Maté argues that a culture that doesn't promote the benefit of soul, spirit and meaning has created a void at the centre of most people's hearts where 'Our consumerist, acquisition-, action-, and image-mad culture only serves to deepen the hole, leaving us emptier than before.'

This fear causes us to reach for anything to get its teeth out of us. I knew I was an addict before I had taken my first drink or drug. My 'addictive personality' was an attempt to escape fear, whether by being excellent in school, texting someone who made me feel like magic until 3 a.m. or controlling my levels of 'full' and 'empty' with over- or undereating. I would do anything for a sense of order in the world, especially as life started to become unfair and things that shouldn't have happened started happening.

Saying, 'I was an addict before I had taken my first drink or drug,' can make people uncomfortable. Sometimes they reassure me that they don't believe I was a bad person, I was a child. Usually this is because people are working under the assumption that addicts are bad people.

People like me are capable of doing selfish, cruel and inconsiderate things. It is usually driven by fear rather than an inherent 'bad' nature. Every impulse that leads us to a harmful act is usually laced with fear, foreboding and a sense of 'I can't handle this, I don't care about the cost.' It doesn't make it OK, but it makes sense. We never grew past the pocket of pain and instead latched onto it, so when it tugs, we don't know what else to do. It doesn't excuse the harm, but it makes the restorative work of change all the more necessary, for our sake and everyone else's.

Fear of rejection

We will never know the true statistics of addiction because our only metrics are people accessing treatment or when it's too late. However, the Forward Trust found that 45 per cent of UK adults have either directly experienced addiction themselves, or know someone close to them who has.[1] Despite this being 22 million people, shame and fear can prevent so many from speaking openly about it. Addiction thrives in secrecy, in the fear of stigma, condemnation or judgement. It grows in the hopelessness that even if you get help, it might not work, or you might be let down or looked down upon for needing it.

There are many barriers in place that prevent people from getting help, even if they ask for it. Addiction is rooted in avoiding pain, and it does not discriminate. However, addicts who are not protected by society will face discrimination.

Alcohol and drug use has been used as a means to blame individuals for circumstances society has engineered; it is acceptable in some contexts and unacceptable in others, depending on tax bracket, employment status, gender and race. Addiction is criminalised in low-income and deprived communities to further marginalise minorities, such as the mass incarcerations of African Americans due to the War on Drugs,[2] a policy started by Richard Nixon in 1971, which continues to this day despite the Global Commission on Drug Policy saying in 2011: 'The global war on drugs has failed, with devastating consequences for individuals and societies around the world.'[3] Alcohol and drug use is used as a tool for anti-immigration scaremongering, using stereotypes like the 'Irish drunk' in England and the USA during the displacement of Irish people due to the great Irish famine[4] and the 'Chinese opium addict' to justify passing the 1882 Chinese Exclusion Act in the USA.[5] Rather than acknowledge that alcohol was used as a tool by colonisers to destroy and control indigenous populations, myths were created to blame them, claiming they were physically different and mentally deficient, unable to drink like 'civilised people'. These lies persist, and fuel stereotypes that addiction is their personal failing, rather than the result of hundreds of years of devastation and dehumanisation passed through the generations. It is a source of judgement towards the rural poor, while it is glamorised for middle-class professionals, rich students and those whose addictions include more socially acceptable ones, like workaholism. We can accept addiction when the addict is doing 'well', whether through recovery, or whether their addiction makes them a tragic figure, who is mourned as a genius who burnt out rather than faded away. Addiction is held in contempt if you're in a personal hell that no one benefits from.

Fear that you don't matter

Sometimes pain seems tolerable when you can assign meaning to it. You can turn your pain into a payoff with creative or monetary value, because otherwise it would just be unfair – or worse, you are different, sick, one of the people that society will stigmatise. To avoid being rejected from society, you work to hide the pain, maybe turn it into something people can enjoy the outcome of, which might prove you're good enough. I wanted to embody this tortured-artist trope, so that it all might mean something.

Comedian and actor Robin Williams described his career as a symptom of his 'please love me syndrome'. Fear, feelings of inadequacy and self-rejection can make you seek fame, acceptance and admiration, when really what you need is to be loved and accepted for who you are. You don't have to be a famous comedian or actor to feel this; you can play this role in the office, in the pub and in your relationships. It's a character that permeates every role in society, from the class clown to the party-girl or the 'funny' friend.

In his essay 'Brief Notes on Staying' (2024), writer Hanif Abdurraqib says:

> The tortured artist is the artist that gets remembered for all time, particularly if they either perish or overcome. But the truth is so many of us are in the middle. So many of us begin tortured and end tortured, with only brief bursts of light in between, and I'd rather have average art and survival than miracles that come at the cost of someone's life

Sometimes you're struggling, life didn't turn out the way you imagined, and you need help that you're scared of asking for and don't want to take. It's hard accepting that you don't have to be in agony or create something timeless for it all to mean something. Or, horrifyingly for me, my alcoholism didn't make me interesting or brilliant. Just a human being, where 'perish' didn't have to be inevitable and 'overcome' didn't have to mean perfection.

Fear of abandonment

When people don't know how to ask for help their behaviours are sometimes called 'attention seeking' or a 'cry for help'. They are the actions of someone who doesn't know how to ask for help directly, has asked for help before and didn't receive it or is wishing people would stop wondering why they keep making 'cries for help' and actually help them.

Being emotionally abandoned when you have low self-esteem can make you believe that being wounded and broken and visibly falling apart is a way to feel worthy of intervention and care. There is a fear of asking for help directly, because young people's feelings aren't always treated with a lot of sincerity, and not everyone knows what it's like to violently hate themselves in the way that makes you open your skin, starve your body and poison yourself.

We're all fucking terrified

The opposite of fear is sometimes said to be faith: to feel the fear and do the scary thing anyway, acting the way you would if you knew everything was going to be OK, whatever the outcome may be in reality. The opposite of fear is also described as certainty, or knowledge. Maybe fear has no easy opposite, but I do know that fear can begin where the facts end and my imagination begins. You have to keep going, and get more evidence of what your life might look like if you tried again, and kept on trying. It's OK to be scared when you are doing something brave – doing what needs to be done when you are scared is what bravery is.

Fear doesn't have to be an individual burden, or a source of shame. It lives behind our eyes and in our guts. It's a lot easier to deal with when you see it for what it is. It is a deeply human thing, sometimes a useful one, connected to instincts that can let us know when we're in harm's way. If you live *in* fear, you get stuck. If you learn to live *with* fear, observing it, you can see what it is trying to tell you and move through it.

We need somewhere safe to talk about our fears. It helps when you have someone who can reassure you that the light at the end of a tunnel isn't a train.

In my first year of music school a group of us were drinking, gathered around a kitchen table. Out of nowhere, someone said, 'Is anyone else finding this really difficult?' A tension that not even the alcohol could touch melted, and we all started talking honestly about how scared we were to be 18 and so desperate to be accepted by a competitive, exclusive and perfectionistic industry. Music school, our unsure futures and our final recitals didn't stop being scary, but at least we knew we weren't alone.

Later, I called my friend Nicholas from a practice room. I asked, 'Do you think I'm an alcoholic?' It was only ever something I'd called myself as a joke before, or to beat anyone who was going to question my behaviour to the punch. He replied immediately, 'I don't know, but I think your drinking is hurting you,' as if he had been waiting to say it for a while.

I didn't get sober for many years after that conversation, but he was the person I spoke to when the fear of things getting worse outweighed them staying the same.

The person to talk to about your fears needs to be someone who knows you, not the version you say you are or pretend to be when you're drunk. It has to be someone who won't encourage feedback loops where you get shut down, or shut yourself down for expressing the darker parts of yourself.

The idea that healing is an individual journey benefits a society that wants to make its failings our fault and frames natural human experiences as something inconvenient

It's not always enough to know why we are afraid. We need to know how to deal with it, and meeting people with the same 'why' can help – people who struggle in the same way we do, have the same rough edges, and who are walking the path we want to. With smokescreens down, there is the safety to be honest, and freedom in experiencing that.

It's often said that connection is the antidote for addiction. It's almost a platitude at this point, but like a lot of platitudes the truth in its roots are found when we put action behind it, rather than simply saying it when there is nothing else to be said. I had reserved the concept of connection for drinking, creating a fast-track, artificial sense of belonging, where I could numb out the reality of being perceived. I believed rigidly that humans were unsafe, would let you down and were built to fuck each other over. It convinced me that complete self-sufficiency was the only safe option, a theory that was supported by a hyper-individualistic society. However, helping and being helped is the cornerstone of being a human. Humans summon tremendous amounts of strength for the sake of other people. They run into burning buildings to save strangers, adopt children, advocate for the oppressed, protect animals, run to people who fall in the street, treat people better than they treat themselves and cling to one another when everything is falling apart. The act of connection requires vulnerability, which can make us recoil for fear of abandonment, rejection or disappointment – but it is also something we can't survive without, as our attempts at going it alone can demonstrate to us.

In twelve-step groups you can be given a coffee by someone who has just broken up with their partner and doesn't know what to do, and sit next to someone who just felt happiness for the first time. You can be greeted by someone who has lost a pregnancy and is confused about how to feel right now, listen to someone who is two minutes sober and be hugged by someone who has finally found comfort in their body. I have been all of these women.

Even if it's just you and one other person, a supportive group is a reminder that we weren't designed to do this alone. If you want to change your crutch, you need something just as strong to replace it, and it's best if it's something loving. There's nothing to fail, because you can't fail at being a human being who is just doing their best. If you're choosing to stay sober in a world that glorifies alcohol you have to find a place where your sobriety fits in. If you want to be in sane and stable relationships when your body is still adjusted to the thrill of a push-and-pull situationship, then you're going to have to create some sane and stable attachments to challenge that. If you want to stop being so fucking sad all the time when society is fixated on the car-crash glamour of personal destruction, then you're going to have to find people who believe that life can be exciting, beautiful and fulfilling alongside the spirals, abysses and sexy depressions.

That idea that a drink might fix it was the only area of my life reserved for hope

When we're scared, hope, optimism and trust feel like abstract concepts. We can aspire to those, and rather than be fearless we can be curious, and have an open mind and a willingness not to run away the second we're required to be honest. We could stay curious that it might work out, rather than damning ourselves with the inevitability that we will fuck it all up. We can be curious about what would happen if we stayed away from the edge of the void, or accept that perhaps the worst won't happen, and even if it does, we might be OK. We can't think fear away. If overthinking made us better, we would all be healed, rather than just cannibalising ourselves with narratives. Action is a way to get out of fear — fixating on fear can allow it to consume us, but when we are paralysed by options, we can line ourselves up with the 'the next right thing' (as they say in twelve-step fellowships).

Talk to people. Ask them what they know about resources, meet-ups, recovery modalities, groups or individuals where you can share truthfully and connect.

Fear can be three things:
- Fear of losing what you have.
- Fear of not getting what you want.
- Fear of being found out.

Fear can mean **F**uck **E**verything **A**nd **R**un, or **F**alse **E**vidence **A**ppearing **R**eal. It can also be **F**ace **E**verything **A**nd **R**ecover.

Outside of acronyms and simplifications, fear is telling us something, and its intel isn't always updated. Fear has protected me from people or places that I had no business being near, but it isn't helpful when I'm believing catastrophic stories I'm telling myself about my fundamental ineptitude. We're braver than we think, and bravery is a muscle we can exercise. Every time we do a courageous thing, it feeds back to us that we are capable, and eventually we begin to believe it. You have probably done some very brave things in your life — you can apply that bravery to accepting help, risking letting someone in, and making small but significant changes with an attitude of 'you are a human who deserves a second chance at this' and not 'you are a fuck-up, destined to perpetually fuck up'.

III. Early Days

If you live in the dark a long time and the sun comes out, you do not cross into it whistling. There's an initial uprush of relief at first, then — for me, anyway — a profound dislocation. My old assumptions about how the world works are buried, yet my new ones aren't yet operational. There's been a death of sorts, but without a few days in hell, no resurrection is possible.

— Mary Karr, *Lit* (2009)

When you know you're doing the right thing, but it still feels like shit. When you've got a bit too comfortable being a maniac, so healthy choices seem insane. When you're saying, 'I don't have to do this, I GET to do this,' with a mouthful of spite and a head full of doubt.

I met my best friend Nicholas, performing the Shostakovich cello and voice duet 'Song of Ophelia' in Glasgow on my twentieth birthday. Fittingly, it led to a bender of melancholy, melodrama and madness. We eventually got kicked out of a

McDonald's at 4 a.m. for trying to start a podcast (our soliloquy), which sent us down the river to my bed, ordering pizzas and ignoring the outside world for days. The fun ended, we sobered up, responsibilities returned, the fear crept in. He said: 'I mean, you stop drinking and then there's just' – he took a long pause – 'everything else.'

It was true on my twentieth birthday, when the 'everything else' was smoothing over drama and cobbling myself back together for the same five-act drama the next weekend, and it was true when I was 25, in 2018, when I decided to change the script and get sober. The relationship I had with the things that changed how I felt had become abusive, and I could no longer keep going back, pretending that what they gave me was love.

I needed something different, something that would last, something I could count on and something that didn't make me piss myself on public transport.

It was astonishing how many of the things I attributed to my anxiety and depression were simply alcohol's effect on my body. Without hangovers sending my serotonin off a cliff, I realised how much stress I'd been putting my body under. I didn't have to worry about unidentified drunken injuries or whether I used a condom last night. I remembered what I said most of the time. My five-year headache felt a bit clearer. I wondered why it had taken me so long to realise this.

But there it was: everything else. I thought I had a drinking problem, when really I had a living-on-planet-earth problem, a feeling-my-feelings problem, a terrified-of-conflict problem, a lost-my-hope-and-burned-out problem, a having-sex-with-men-I-hated problem, a self-hatred problem. I also had a drinking problem, and addressing that made all of these things very loud.

Alongside the benefits, my body was trying to work out a new rhythm, so I was exhausted. My emotions were prickling like a toothache. Sharp stabs of shame would slice through benign conversations or at the supermarket checkout. I became a dopamine goblin, trying to suck a hit out of anything that might feel good, and I became emotionally dependent on the dark triad of caffeine, nicotine and sugar. I wanted a hotline to my body, to know when I needed to eat and sleep, then I remembered that's what hunger and tiredness were. I felt like the receptors for love and kindness didn't exist in my heart, and when good things came my way I couldn't connect with them and transfer them into happiness. I was numb and felt everything at once. You don't expect the best thing you've ever done to hurt so much.

When I realised I had been treating my mental-health issues with alcohol and drugs, they resurfaced and confronted me in ways that I didn't expect, now that I was supposed to be on a 'healing journey'. Part of the healing was realising how bad I'd let it get, and how lonely I was. I didn't know how to talk to people any more, so I became reclusive and paranoid, plagued not just by the nagging thought that my friends secretly hated me, but by a worldview where I had missed my chance at happiness and everyone was out to get me.

My early sobriety experience, in the spring of 2018, was feeling everything I'd ever avoided feeling, and new feelings I didn't know existed, while trying not to get kicked out of my master's degree in opera at Yale after my less-than-stellar performance in *The Magic Flute*. I had been awarded a full scholarship – on paper, the greatest chance I had ever been given. A perfect 'I'll-show-them-*all*' moment. My recently ex-boyfriend, Kweku, had broken up with me just before I accepted my place at Yale. We met on Tinder in 2016, matching as I passed through his town in New Jersey on my way to New York from Indiana, where I was living at the time. We didn't meet in person, but continued to text every day, his name coming up on my screen hitting a vein every time. We eventually met in Memphis, when I advanced to the finals of a competition and asked if he wanted to meet me there. I placed third in the competition but didn't care, I had created a fairy tale – I was falling in love with someone I'd met in an improbable way, in a romcom montage of eating pancakes in a hotel room and laughing while dismantling a coat hanger to open a bottle of wine because there was no corkscrew. The fantasy transferred into a fizzy and fun long-distance relationship, until I started drunkenly accusing him of cheating on me whenever I felt insecure, making our nightly phone calls an excuse to cry about the pain of my past, and blaming him for my unhappiness when he had shown me nothing but kindness. After a year or so of this, in mid-2017 he ended it with a not-a-bang-but-a-whimper phone call where he simply said, 'I'm tired.'

    I thought getting into Yale would be a *Legally Blonde*-style vignette. I would get to say, 'What, like it's hard?' when he found out. As it happens, it actually was very hard, but not for the reasons I thought it would be. I was sober now, haemorrhaging money on a downtown apartment, and living on a mattress on the floor, claiming I was a 'minimalist'. I was absolutely incapable of taking care of myself, and couldn't believe that was my responsibility; I couldn't even keep a houseplant alive. Having a human body seemed like such a massive inconvenience, so I overworked it, threw myself into any distraction – extra ushering shifts at the concert hall where I worked part-time, doing a lifetime of errands in one day, and watching twenty-two-part documentaries on the

Cold War and Yugoslavia, taking notes as if there would be a quiz at the end. That seemed easier than making a meal or drinking a glass of water. It often does for burned-out overachievers.

Two roads diverged in a newly sober wood

Me and Nicholas used to have a mantra: 'Vodka or yoga: pick one, give it all you've got.' That was my attitude to life: your choices existed at diametrically opposing ends. My choice in early recovery was whether to stay at Yale or drop out. I could stay and get my degree, get famous (potentially break down with the pressure), or drop out, go home, work on the farm, live a quiet life of chopping wood and carrying water (potentially break down over the fact that I am simply not a farmer).

I stayed at Yale, but the conditions of staying were making space for the things I needed to get better. Whatever I did, whichever choice I made, I was going to put recovery first, and give *that* all I'd got. It started practically. I let professors know I was struggling and actually told them I was dyslexic, rather than trying to prove something by not accepting extra time in written exams. I took the suggested breaks for rehearsals and spent time with friends who weren't going to ask hopefully if I was going to drink tonight. I tried to start running, because I thought that was what sober people did, and discovered I'm built for comfort, not speed. I resisted picking up and smoking a cigarette butt I saw on the pavement. I made a meal and did the dishes.

The days went on. I got these strange spots around my mouth that I didn't even get in puberty, my energy swung between manic and non-existent – but I didn't drink. My luteal phase got so much more intense. Maybe it always had been that bad, I just never noticed it before, being too accustomed to feeling terrible all the time. I took my make-up off every night. I consistently brushed my teeth. I kept asking no one in particular, 'Do I have to do these stupid little things every fucking day?' No one in particular replied, 'Yes.' It wasn't grand gestures or dramatic release; it was the daily devotions that one day would become normal parts of a routine. That semester they sealed the windows of the music building, because a student jumped to their death. I cried for them, and realised how close I was to being them.

At twenty-eight days sober I walked past a Mexican restaurant with a half-finished margarita on the table. This immobilised me, not just because there are people who can leave a drink unfinished, but because the sticky, sugared mouth of the glass was singing a siren song of 'no one would know'. On the one hand, I considered that I might have learned enough self-control to only drink one, or (for fuck's sake) half a margarita. On the other, I knew I couldn't drink just one, and didn't want to. Even imagining drinking one, I was already fantasising about how far I could take it, how far from myself I could get. I left it, and called a woman from my twelve-step group, who I knew would hear me describe how hard it was not to drink abandoned cocktails on the side of the street, and nod with identification on the other end of the phone.

What's hard for other people might be easy for us, and what's easy for other people is really difficult in early recovery

What I didn't know at the time was that it would not feel this way forever. The early days of sobriety, with their second puberty, delayed adolescence and civil war with your brain, are not a punishment, but an area of exploration. They are growing pains, as opposed to the pain of staying the same. You realise what needs to change in your environment, relationships and lifestyle, and make steps towards creating a life you can tolerate, even enjoy, that doesn't require an ejector seat. You get to build yourself up and experience your agency with your daily choices. What you're running from catches up with you, and you have to move gradually and compassionately, even if it feels like walking in fog.

However, when you have a propensity to be hard on yourself, working through something gradually and compassionately doesn't always come easily.

There's a saying that the alcoholic is the failed perfectionist. By its nature, perfectionism sets an unachievable standard that guarantees misery. When the only alternative to complete failure is absolute perfection, you can become a control freak, or withdrawn and unable to start literally anything because the tyrant in your head will condemn you for even having the notion. Self-sabotage and self-destruction can feel like an appropriate self-punishment for the crushing sense of internal failure that inherently exists within perfectionism, and the only other option if perfection isn't possible. No one is more self-critical, bound by unreasonably high standards, unwilling to ask for help and sensitive to perceived failures than perfectionists who self-medicate with chemical oblivion. This violent self-soothing can feel like the only relief for this inescapable internal struggle. You don't want to go slow, take it easy, try new things and potentially fail – you want to be perfect. Only that will treat your dismal self-esteem.

This mindset makes early recovery an uncomfortable experience. You feel further away than ever from your perceived idea of how and where you should be. If you've gone to a dark place from which you didn't think you would return, you've developed life skills from hell, and proved you can survive anything. When building towards something new, you are confronted with the life skills that you didn't get to practise while you were trying to survive, like tolerating a negative emotion rather than taking a dramatic action against it, taking care of basic needs and being honest with yourself and others.

I knew how to work hard and do difficult things, because being an opera singer was hard work and very difficult. I worked at it until it came easily to me. What was difficult for me now was moving out of survival, and into a bit of structure and routine that worked for me, where I'd eat some meals at a regular time, sleep rather than pass out, be on time, commit to a schedule with reasonable demands and not drink or do drugs. My hard work now was learning the skills of everyday living that I'd missed out on along the road of my self-destruct mission. I had to find out how to function with the material I had to work with, and by no one else's standards. I wasn't contorting myself into a society I found nonsensical, but looking for ways to use my energy and effort in ways I felt were worthwhile.

Whatever you find difficult in early recovery, even if it is a 'normal' task, is simply a new challenge, and it is naturally difficult, because you don't have any practice at it yet. Sometimes you have to do the hard thing a few more times and hope it gets easier, to embody the version of yourself you can live with – and not just a version of what you thought success was, where you are either perfect or a failure. If you've spent a long time feeling like there is something deeply, deeply wrong with you, shame is a stubborn belief that needs a bit more than twenty-eight days to change. You can't expect to master your new challenges immediately, but you can be willing to try on a day-by-day basis. Taking things one day at a time is the hardest work to do if you feel like you will only be satisfied with a perfect outcome, but it's also how recovery works.

Smashing a box of wine isn't a mental-health day and sending your ex nudes isn't self-care

I never paid attention to the case for sobriety that alcohol was poison and we shouldn't poison ourselves, because I didn't have enough self-esteem to consider myself someone who shouldn't be poisoned. But as I walked away from that margarita, I started to recognise that I was choosing self-esteem over dopamine.

Self-esteem is present when we value and perceive ourselves in a way that acknowledges our humanity, dignity and right to be here. When the discomfort of early recovery drags you into the present, you can realise how low your opinion of yourself is. You start to notice where you undercut or betray yourself. Feelings of inadequacy, jealousy and envy can make you hate your loved ones and want to impress your enemies.

Self-esteem can be trapped in the prison walls of shame – the salted soil of your self-worth, which nothing can grow on top of; the hollow rattle at the end of a twisted corridor; the thing inside that says, 'You are unacceptable, no one is going to love you – take a drink.' Shame is not embarrassment, which can motivate us into making a healthy change. Shame wants us to stay down, to not take ourselves seriously or treat ourselves with any level of regard, so we can keep it company.

We aren't taught how to develop and nurture self-esteem in

any direct way. We feel like it might come from external validation or self-improvement, believing hopefully that this will feel like enough. We can prove ourselves or get as much praise as we can, but if we are piling it on top of something that we don't believe about ourselves, it triggers that feeling of emptiness after we receive and reject a compliment, the fear that we've deceived someone. There's no amount of external validation that will improve our self-esteem unless we are connecting and improving our relationship with ourselves.

Our choice to brave early recovery is a foundation to grow self-esteem, and all the efforts we make towards it strengthens it. However, acting in your own best interests is hard when you're struggling with self-hatred – which, for me, made it all the more frustrating when people said things like, 'Take care of yourself,' and, 'Be gentle with yourself,' as if I'd ever done anything gently or cared for myself in my entire life.

The term self-care just seemed to appear on the internet one day, and it wasn't long before it was framed as a symptom of millennial self-obsession, while simultaneously being used as a capitalist marketing strategy to sell us an idea of rest and restoration as a commodity, rather than treating the source of why we are so depleted in the first place.

The concept has existed philosophically for decades – Socrates and Foucault both explored how practising taking care of yourself is a necessary part of being human, for the good of ourselves, our community and the world. It was adopted as a medical concept in the 1950s, as a set of simple principles for patients to prevent or manage conditions. During the late 1960s and 1970s Civil Rights Movement it evolved into a political action, necessary for Black communities who were medically discriminated against and dismissed by the healthcare system, and who faced daily hostility based on the fact of their existence. The focus on investing time and effort into themselves was critical for activists in their resistance, organisation, mobilisation and creation of social change, in an environment that opposed their human dignity.

Self-care is acknowledging the necessity of investing in our survival beyond just staying alive, and making the changes to accommodate the results we want to see. It is prioritising our safety. It is admin, sleep, hygiene, taking physical and emotional rest, household tasks, enrichment, therapy, mindfulness and budgeting. It might not always be comfortable to practise self-care, because we may have adapted to make ourselves comfortable in chaos, on the edge, outside of our bodies before. To care for something is to nurture it and nourish its growth. Self-care must treat our needs, rather than obscure them with more comfortable, short-acting pleasures – as much as I love little-treat culture, that is self-soothing and necessary (especially in early recovery), we also have to build the muscles for something more sustainable to treat the deeper issues. The nutrients are in the doing of it, not in it being done as another thing ticked off an oppressive to-do list. It is as powerful as the intention behind it, and how it is used to increase resilience.

Self-care builds self-esteem, and early recovery is a perfect place to incorporate it, as we are rebuilding the way we see ourselves by the way we treat ourselves. We can build from the place of brushing our teeth and taking our make-up off, then surprise ourselves by what we are actually capable of if we are willing to challenge ourselves. It is present and grows when we are valuing our integrity above what people might think of us, being honest rather than palatable, engaging in friendships as an equal participant so that we begin to believe we are just as worthy as anyone else, and showing up for each other, even when we don't want to but it is what we need to do right now.

None of these things happens overnight, and you can't expedite the process. They come in the small, daily efforts, where self-esteem is built in esteemable acts.

Putting yourself first doesn't mean putting others last – it means being the best version of yourself for other people

My friend Kirstin got sober in the COVID lockdown. She describes how 'I lived in a flat with three flights of stairs. I imagined myself falling down the stairs drunk, and breaking my neck. If I was going to die in a fall, it would be falling off the side of a yacht in Monaco. I didn't want to die alone, so after six months of relapsing, I thought I would take everyone's suggestions, really do them, and if they didn't work, I'd just get a one-way flight to Monaco.'

Kirstin, at the time of writing, has been sober for five years, and is just back from a solo trip to Zanzibar, where she managed not to fall off any yachts.

'COVID kept me sober at first, because the pubs shut. In the beginning I did really simple and gentle stuff – watching a lot of *Real Housewives of New York*, rearranging my bookshelves, taking care of my physical health properly for the first time, eating, sleeping, flossing. I wasn't trying to impress my mum or my colleagues, I was doing it for me. Once I started to take care of myself for myself, things started happening. I wanted to live. Shame started falling off. Change happened, so I kept doing it.'

Taking care of ourselves can feel like a selfish endeavour, but the connection to ourselves allows for a connection to other people.

Kirstin continues, 'I always called people when I went to the shop, to hold me accountable to not buy alcohol. We talked about normal stuff – bills, fears, halving our problems by sharing them. I used to abandon myself so much, either by chasing men or doing drugs to hang out with people who didn't even know my second name. Even though I knew what the drugs would do to me, even though I knew where they would take me, I felt like I had to do them so I'd be loved and accepted.'

When it comes to the early days, Kirstin believes in the importance of prioritising recovery, to stop the constant loop of ignoring our needs.

'If I'm not putting myself first, I'm putting myself last. In all the self-abandonment of trying to get someone to love me, it's self-harm. I can't do that any more, when I know I can love myself so well. Things can change for the better – we all start to grow up at some point. I visited one of my old friends recently, and our old coke den is now a nursery.'

Three tiny things

Sometimes we don't have to do more things, we can simply try to do a few things well.

'Three tiny things' are non-negotiable parts of the day that nurture our sense of who we are and show us we are valuing ourselves. My three tiny things were initially to take my make-up off, brush my teeth and read something. It's a mixture of discipline and compassion, because both are required to make a change.

Think of three tiny things you can do every day that you need to do, but don't always want to, and frame it in a loving way.

I have more than three things now, which operate simply as a part of a flexible routine, but if I had started with the number I have now I would have been overwhelmed by the prospect of failing them, and wouldn't have bothered. So building them gradually wasn't a cop-out, but a necessary start.

My early recovery experience was realising that most of the good things in my life are on the other side of something I initially didn't want to do. I didn't want to go to church basements on a Saturday morning, make coffee and talk to strangers in a circle of plastic folding chairs, but it's where I learned how to show up for myself and others, look someone in the eye and commit to a process without planning my escape from it. I didn't want to do the step-work and therapy worksheets. I didn't want to hoover my room, clean my dishes, be honest, get out of bed, move my body and calm my mind. But on a day-to-day basis, I did, and that's where the change happened.

You can't think your way into right action, but you can act your way into right thinking. I have been surprised over and over again at what I have been able to give myself and those around me with this simple phrase, by simply making a start and going forward with things that are in alignment with who I am and who I am becoming.

HALT

HALT is for when someone is walking in front of you too slowly and you wonder whether it's legal to pull their ponytail, an ambiguous text makes you hit 'block' on a best friend or the world is ending because you missed the Tube by eight seconds and the next train isn't for nine minutes. It takes the smallest pin prick to burst a balloon. It's low-level yet persistent overstimulation rather than catastrophic events that are more likely to make you want to explode, and sometimes you're more likely to drink over the molehills rather than the mountains. When the check-engine light is flashing, you could put a piece of black tape over it, or you could ask yourself if you are:

Hungry
Angry
Lonely
Tired

If you can identify one of these as the answer, it won't solve a complex issue (though it has made me realise an issue is a lot simpler than I thought), but it can stop you from acting in a way that will make it a lot worse. When hunger, anger, loneliness or tiredness render you emotionally vulnerable, it leaves you defenceless when the inevitable annoyances of everyday living are coming at you from every angle, which, when you live in London, is often.

As much as I have a fantasy of being a reclusive bohemian who doesn't sleep or require sustenance, I can be a bohemian with a few friends who also eats meals and goes to bed once in a while. Having HALT is having something to consider before I intoxicate myself on a feeling, or do something extreme to unplug from being a highly sensitive person. It is a check-in before I throw it all away, when I just need to eat something.

Safe and trusted connections with others are fundamental to building a meaningful life and necessary for your mental health

Nurturing ourselves is crucial and a huge focus of early recovery, but we can't ignore the deeply human need to be seen and accepted for who we are. We've already covered accepting help when us-against-the-world becomes a losing battle, and honestly letting someone know what we are going through, so we realise we are not alone. The importance of other people doesn't end there.

Continuing to build safe connections with others prevents that type of loneliness where we slowly shut down and disappear. The existence of other people often isn't enough; if it was, we could still be doing lines with strangers in the bathroom. We need to develop closeness and trust with others.

I had never enjoyed being who I was and, being sober, I had to be that every day. I'd developed a version of myself to hide the more complex areas of myself, *The Lauren Show* – a protective, performative casing from the horror of being known. *The Lauren Show* was never bullied, never spent all day thinking about what people were thinking of her, and didn't have any soft parts. When *The Lauren Show* was playing, nothing could touch me, and so nothing could hurt.

Connecting to people in early recovery can be uncomfortable. We might not want to admit when it's hard, or trust that someone will be available or able to hold our more truthful expressions of ourselves. We don't want to feel like a burden so we use our troubles as content and anecdotes. We can package them in careful ways, and present versions of ourselves for consideration, making it seem like we are being transparent. We can create a hologram of ourselves, where people will have an idea of us, but never the reality of us.

We do not heal alone; we heal our wounds through intimacy with ourselves, and with others. There will be someone in your life who will be safe to build trust with, who already is or may become a trusted person. In early recovery we must go where it's warm, and build those bonds with time. With this trusted person you don't have to fix each other, you just have to be there. Sometimes with solution-orientated conversations, and sometimes just a hand to hold in the dark, knowing we can go to them and not receive any judgement or condemnation. Even when the rest of the world misunderstands us, no matter how many people tell us we're overreacting or that we should try having just one when we've made it clear we're trying to abstain, knowing that we are loved by someone we trust, or are beginning to trust, is a safe place.

Building a life you can tolerate starts with building a day you can tolerate – one day at a time starts in the morning

When the word 'morning' has been synonymous with the word 'doom' for many years, it might be an area of the day you don't want to give any attention to, aside from working out how to pretend the uncomfortable tear between sleeping and waking isn't happening. Mornings can feel like a punitive space, reserved for people whose temperament is suited to them, and while there are some people who are more biologically suited to mornings, everyone can benefit from the non-punishing discipline of committing to a simple routine, doing it, then choosing to do it the next day. This builds self-esteem, because you are taking the commitments you make to yourself seriously. It cannot be an impossible standard to hold yourself in contempt over if you can't fulfil it; it is simply a few things in place that create the space to catch and gather yourself, to set a foundation. Here you can temperature-check your mood, see what you need and create a sense of routine to strengthen your decisions in the rest of the day.

A morning routine was the first structure that I didn't want to rebel against, because I got to decide what it was. We get to decide what matters to us and dedicate time to it. It creates time to be before it's time to do, and reiterates the importance of that. We can stretch, meditate, do something that engages our brain, take quiet moments or listen to music to set the tone for the day. It's something uniquely ours and can be flexible, changing for whatever we require, day to day, or season by season. The most important thing is that it is useful to you, and the sort of day you want to have. It was a compassionate entry to observing where I am playing a role in my suffering. I can greet myself gently and enjoy some quiet before exposing myself to the demands and horrors inside my phone, or I can wake up, roll over, scroll jadedly for fifteen minutes and feel a bit shit about my life before my day has even started.

If the first attempt falls off the rails, I try to remember that you can restart your day at absolutely any point, but however and whenever I wake up, I ask myself, 'Where do I want to put my effort and energy today?'

It helps to have reminders of why you want to do this, why you are still doing it, even when it's hard – especially when it's hard. When you set the intention for a better life, it wasn't enough to just want it. It's easy to forget the reasons you want to stay sober when the feelings from the last shame spiral aren't as intense and old rationalisations come back. If you want the outcome, you have to want the process just as much.

Breaking free of embedded patterns and old ideas takes awareness and effort. These things don't go away in an instant, and the counter-effort is going to need a strong foundation and continued use before it feels easy. You know how to do hard things, you have done very hard things – and the hardest, most important thing you'll ever do is unlearning the conscious and unconscious maladaptive ways you learned in order to cope with the world, and breaking down your defence mechanisms that have been baked in from childhood and adolescence. This process is stepping into an unknown rather than returning to a 'before' – but it is returning to the truth of you, before you had to contort yourself. If you are patient with yourself, what's on the other side is living in a sense of freedom in who you are.

PART II

Looking inwards – how to experience yourself when you've spent most of your life trying to escape yourself.

IV. Senses

By the time I was thirteen, I had divorced my body. Like a bitter divorced parent, I accepted that our collaboration was mandatory. I needed her and hated her all the more for it.

— Melissa Febos, *Girlhood* (2021)

When you struggle to connect to your own body, never mind the world around you. When you struggle with either feeling too much of everything or nothing. When you want to connect to your senses in a way that doesn't make you want to explode.

Like most teenagers from the remote countryside, I passed my driver's test when I was 17. It was non-negotiable if you wanted any sort of freedom. A few months later, I met a tractor on a hairpin bend and flipped the car off the road. In that moment before time stopped, and my brain acted reflexively to minimise the chance of dying. Before the crash I was listening to *Rodeo* by Aaron Copland. I could smell the straw on the wellies in the back seat, and the deep green of the rain-soaked trees by the road almost had a metallic glow as my headlights flashed past them. But I couldn't hear the music when the car turned on its side and things started smashing, the wellies became just another thing being thrown about in the chaos, and everything was black and white. Sound returned a few minutes later when I opened my eyes and realised I was alive, hanging by the tense pull of my seatbelt. My thoughts returned, like blood through a stab wound, horrifying and gradual. When the adrenalin of being suspended in a life-or-death moment faded, the world filled in around me again, and it was loud. Experiencing the world newly sober sometimes felt like I was coming out of that totalled car, wondering how I had survived, worried about what I was going to do with the wreckage and what I was going to tell my dad.

At six months sober things were starting to feel slightly easier, or at least familiar. Dominic, the man I'd started seeing just before I got sober, hadn't left me, Yale hadn't kicked me out, I'd spent the summer in Colorado singing for Central City Opera and I only had three meltdowns while doing my tax return (it was previously five). My therapist suggested we work on some grounding techniques to deal with my anxiety around returning to the rehearsal room for my next performance. She asked me if I've heard of 'Five, four, three, two, one'. I told her I'd seen at least an infographic a week asking me to name five things I can see, four things I can hear, three things I can touch, two things I can smell and one thing I can taste. I wanted her to give me a more complicated one, a special and secret one only she can tell me.

She asked me if I'd ever tried it, and I admitted no, though I had told many other people to. I said it seemed too simple to work. She told me grounding techniques were by their nature simple, because they are to be used in times of distress. Like giving yourself a hug, kissing your shoulder or breathing in for four, holding for four, exhaling for four and holding that for four on repeat when your brain is telling you there is an imminent threat to your existence.

Again, I told her I knew how to do box breathing – I taught that in my singing and breathwork workshops.

She asked me again: 'Do you ever do it yourself?'

I had to admit, again, that I didn't. But I thought that by being a singer, an actress and a woman who'd had sex with strangers, I had already mastered connecting to my body. I used it to make music and create chemistry with stage partners that could be seen from the cheap seats.

She asked me how I felt in my body right now, when I was just existing, and not putting on a show. I told her, 'I don't feel my body right now; when I do it's usually a problem.' When I feel my body and its sensations, I remember things. Like when I had vocal coaching with a famous French mélodie répétiteur – we were doing resonance exercises, feeling the sound waves from the vocal folds vibrate, then focusing that sensation in different parts of the body. The involuntary experience of letting the resonance spin in my skull reminded me of the other involuntary experiences my body felt – panic, dizziness, palpitations, the symptoms of reliving a traumatic memory. Then I couldn't open my mouth, because somewhere in my body I was physically revisiting being forced to my knees by a man I had tried to forget. I called them 'memory-zaps' – they would surface and burst across my brain, like it wanted to make sure I didn't forget. I had a strange relationship with remembering.

Once, when I received the news of a friend's death, I ran into the snowstorm outside without a jacket. It was only after half an hour of being in the snow, and I felt my body say, 'You're cold,' that I remembered what I had lost.

My body felt like a haunted attic: when the trapdoor opens the dust moves, and horrors beyond my comprehension start to make the floorboards creak.

As the session continued we started talking about the things I usually would only tell people when I was drunk with my high heels in my hands, sobbing as someone tried to get me in a taxi. I felt my palms get sweaty, the backs of my eyes pulsed with a headache and something inside me said 'run'.

I found myself in the first defence mechanism I used as a child. I pictured myself walking through the winding corridor of a castle, running my hand along the ragged stone walls. This dissociation palace protected me from a lot of things I was too young to understand, like why a tutor would tell a child he loved them in a way no one else could – that's why he was doing what he did, and I couldn't tell anyone because they wouldn't understand.

My therapist asked if now was a good time to practise a grounding exercise. The adrenalin stopped saying 'run' and started saying 'fight'.

But I humoured her, and we did it out loud. I tried to describe the colours of a stock image of a woodland scene on the wall. I couldn't remember the words for a plug socket. I heard the tick of the clock. I tasted mint and coffee. I stopped spinning out.

It couldn't be that easy, I said.

She said, 'It isn't; this is a safe and controlled environment with someone you've built trust with. The hard part is doing it out there, and knowing what to do and doing it when it's hard.' Like alcohol, dissociation had served its purpose, and protected me when I wasn't ready to feel and face certain things, but it wasn't sustainable, or the life hack I thought it was.

She suggested I try this technique often, even when I wasn't in distress, so my brain had a worn-in pathway it could use reflexively. I said I wasn't sure if it would work.

She replied: 'You can't say something doesn't work until you've given it everything you've got. And if it doesn't work then, you try something different.'

Over the weeks of practising objectively naming things I sensed, I started to notice more. I would be struck by the pastel colours of the houses on my street, each with their own loafy sofa on the porch where children played, students read and people met to play cards. My eyes were drawn in by the miraculous fact that trees had leaves – kaleidoscopic patterns of them – reaching over me on either side of the pavement as I walked to work. I didn't know I had freckles until I could look myself in the eye. I had a spiritual experience noticing for the first time how honey actually tasted, and wondered how something that magical could exist. I played my friends songs I'd listened to for years and asked, 'Has that bass line always been there? It sounds amazing.'

We started dialectical behaviour therapy (DBT), a modality designed for people who feel intense emotions, which covers distress tolerance, emotional regulation, interpersonal effectiveness and mindfulness, with a lot of acronyms. I realised that TIPP really worked for me – using **T**emperature, **I**ntense exercise, **P**aced breathing and **P**aired muscle relaxation when an overwhelming feeling made me want to reach for a sharp object.

When I was overcome by an urge I felt I couldn't control, I could shock my way out of it by dunking my face in iced water, doing star-jumps or, on the easier days, simply popping an ice cube in my mouth. The intense shift in temperature redirected my brain away from what was consuming me. They weren't sustainable, long-term solutions, but they were expanding my window of tolerance to life as I built resilience.

Things still overwhelmed me, my brain still played the evolutionary trick of trying to protect me from a tiger when the bus was just too hot and full of bus smells and I wanted to run into the forest because someone brushed up against me. But I had something to do about it.

Esmé Weijun Wang says in *The Collected Schizophrenias* (2019), 'To say this prayer – burn this candle – perform this ritual – create this salt or honey jar – is to have something to do when it seems that nothing can be done.'

Grounding, breathing, praying and mindfulness exercises became my ritual. They still are my anchor to the present, a reminder that just because I am overwhelmed doesn't mean I am not going to be OK.

The universe of the past is happening inside me right now

Sometimes you can feel like there's a stranger in your body, and it's you. You maybe once believed you processed your trauma by obliterating it with alcohol and drugs, but that just leaves it frozen in time. As you dry out, it thaws out. The word trauma is taken from the Greek word for wound. If after an injury your pain is taken seriously and you are given appropriate treatment with the necessary aftercare, the wound will heal well. It will integrate gradually into the experience of your body, even if it changes how you relate to it. If the wound is belittled, ignored, or the necessary treatment isn't available, you find yourself having to create ways to work around it. You'll hide it or try to destroy the pain signals it's giving you, simply in order to keep going. When you get sober, you're finally feeling it all.

I convinced myself I wasn't traumatised because I didn't seem to have specific triggers, apart from the least sinister song of all time, 'Mr Blue Sky' – the unfortunate soundtrack to the first time a man I loved and feared in equal measure hit me. Largely I would get activated unexpectedly, for no apparent reason, at any time, under any circumstances. I told myself I was making a big deal out of nothing, because I wasn't a legitimately traumatised person. They had actual triggers.

Not everyone has a list of things they can neatly package into a box marked 'trigger'. Sometimes the particulars of a traumatic situation become the centre of a spiderweb, which branches outwards and gets blurry. If you've been through a traumatic event involving a jagged knife, if you don't process it, your brain starts recognising the butter knife as a potential threat. Then spoons start to blur out into the messy swamp of 'things that remind me of the worst thing that ever happened to me'. Before long the cutlery drawer becomes a source of fear. In many of my traumatic events I was naked and vulnerable, so I couldn't be naked in front of other people while sober. Then I couldn't wear things in public that showed my skin. Then even getting undressed for the shower felt like an ordeal.

It's not that I didn't have triggers, I was just drunk most of my adult life, and spent the time when I wasn't avoiding absolutely everything. What's more, my brain had just continued to generalise, until everything felt like a threat.

When your brain has become too skilled at dissociating and generalising, you can utilise grounding techniques alongside 'stimulus discrimination' – separating the present from the past. When activated you can attempt to identify a stimulus, no matter how vague, and separate it from the past using your senses to ground yourself undeniably in the present moment. Ensuring and assuring your safety, you begin to realise that the spoon in the cutlery drawer is not the same weapon that almost took your life, getting undressed for the shower doesn't mean you're going to be raped and not everyone is going to take their rage out on you because you made a human error.

When you have the type of trauma where you'd much prefer to give yourself alcohol poisoning than risk experiencing anything that might remind you of your past, external stimuli aren't the only risks. Living in your own body is its own minefield.

> Traumatised people chronically feel unsafe inside their bodies: The past is alive in the form of gnawing interior discomfort. Their bodies are constantly bombarded by visceral warning signs, and, in an attempt to control these processes, they often become expert at ignoring their gut feelings and in numbing awareness of what is played out inside. They learn to hide from their selves.
> – Bessel van der Kolk, *The Body Keeps the Score: Brain, Mind and Body in the Healing of Trauma* (2014)

As we return to our body and step out of dissociation, a decade's worth of tears can be waiting for us. For all the things we belittled and normalised, for all the screams we kept in our throat because someone said if we told anyone bad things would happen, for all the times we said yes but meant no because it was safer this way even if the cost was our dignity, for all the deaths that didn't make sense, for all the times we were let down by people who knew better, for all the times we were taken advantage of in blackout.

We may need support to integrate our past in a safe environment, so we can one day imagine a life without it making a fist around our throat. We need the trauma books and peer support, to sob through yin yoga sessions, take the time with different therapy modalities, breathe and sing and exist in our living, breathing body one millimetre at a time. We need to hear people say, 'That happened to me, too,' and see that they are OK now.

Time takes time, and what's normal for you might not be normal for everyone. It might not even be normal for you in a year's time. To this day I get hypnagogic hallucinations, a somewhat common symptom of PTSD: I wake up convinced there are spiders in the sheets and blood on the walls, and have to guide myself to the point where I can grab a tether to reality and ground myself. It's a process, and I've never judged or shamed myself into making it go more quickly.

Stepping into your senses can be the beginning of integration

Much like a relationship you find yourself shrinking in, where you don't know your favourite colour any more because you've had to sacrifice so much of yourself, an unhealthy relationship with alcohol destroys your experience of yourself. The diminishing returns, the things you forfeit to keep it and the numbness it encourages not only warps your sense of self, but your senses.

As unwelcome an awakening stepping out of dissociation can be, eventually you can start to experience the world around you more. In recovery this is an opportunity to discover very basic things about yourself, outside of survival mode. When you learn how to live safely inside yourself, you can feel safer with others and in the world at large – the change on the inside encourages you to change the very conditions of your life.

When I crashed into recovery I literally had no idea what I liked or was interested in. Connecting to your senses can help you find out what you actually enjoy, and direct you towards interests, pleasures and causes that you can pursue for their own sake. It is not only necessary work, but a foundation to work out exactly what lights you up, relaxes you and excites you that isn't alcohol or drugs.

A crucial part of sobriety is working out ways to wind down from stress outside of the old 'nothing-to-be-stressed-about-if-you-destroy-everything-you-love!' sabotage refrain. Connecting with our senses finds avenues that feel good for us. Restoring our relationship to our senses in a safe way helps us restore our relationship to ourselves. It is also a reminder that it's OK to feel things. It's actually quite good to feel things sometimes.

Sound

When your depth of feeling makes you the sort of person who can be moved to tears by three bars of a cello solo, you know intrinsically how powerfully music can be utilised to process what is going on in the underworld of your human experience.

Music also allows you to turn away from feelings that you're getting sick of, like listening to soothing music when you're full of rage or listening to music that drives hard when you're feeling sluggish.

A lot of people start listening to the music they listened to as a teenager when they get sober; the melodrama matches the feelings they're returning to. You can use music to process, indulge or reflect on an era, though it's best to avoid listening to songs you did fistfuls of drugs to, so it doesn't fall into romanticisation. You can call your soul back and massage your skeleton with your flesh through movement. You can make playlists for different moods, find a new genre you haven't explored before, risk liking something that isn't cool, share it with other people, make the effort to see live music, sing, hum, recite poetry, watch films in different languages, do a guided meditation, enjoy silence and hear things with the intention of listening.

Taste

Never having a lot of money or time meant that I had never really considered food as something more than an inconvenience, or something else with which to create an artificial sense of wholeness. So few of us got out of the early-2000s' obsession with dieting unscathed, so food may still feel like the enemy of thinness. If you've been living on the edge, your body is flooded with adrenalin, which switches off your hunger cues.

Sobriety gives you an unfiltered view of taste. As an adult you get to decide what you do and do not like. While the blueprints of calorie counting, abusing MyFitnessPal and seeing food as an insult to your body are worn in hard, you can work to get to a place where you acknowledge food as a nourishing, necessary and often enjoyable thing.

Cooking was the first thing I'd dismiss as unnecessary, and I didn't have a lot of skill around it because I simply hadn't done it in my decline of taking care of myself. I had to schedule time for it and see it as a valid use of my time. Its validity is highlighted when we consider the intimacy of cooking for friends, and the grounding joy in cooking food from your heritage, culture or a memory that doesn't hurt.

Taste doesn't even have to be about food. There is nothing more delicious than a lover's sweat, or a really good Diet Coke.

Smell

In 2019, a year after the ill-fated production of *The Magic Flute*, the god-awful soundtrack to my entry to sobriety, I was back on-stage at the Shubert Theatre, performing my first sober principal role: Tatyana in *Eugene Onegin*. After having her heart broken and her innocence stolen, she ends the opera with a rich husband, while the man who rejected her goes insane (and, honestly, good for her). It's an exposed and challenging task, to embody a woman's coming-of-age through the most painful junction of her life, but that's what opera singers know how to do. We also know how to avoid a cold, which involves 90 per cent alcohol hand sanitiser on every prop table. I once wondered if snorting it would count as a relapse.

Scents throw us in or out of a moment instantly and without our effort. Smelling Joop! Jump reminds me of my first crush. Lemon wipes remind me of one time being so hungover I didn't have the energy to shower, so I tried to wash myself with them before leaving the house, thinking they were baby wipes. Hand sanitiser reminds me of, well, you get the idea. On the other hand, smelling oil paints reminds me of my grandmother, who painted passionately even though she never had the option to apply to art school like she wanted. Cinnamon reminds me of baking with my sister. Palo santo reminds me of my best friend.

We can utilise this. I carried some scents, oils and perfumes for when I was overwhelmed and upset. I was extremely sceptical of this when it was suggested to me, but I was convinced when I actually experienced overriding those powerful memories with another one. It also made me feel like a Victorian woman with smelling salts, and I enjoyed the drama of that.

Sight

I didn't know what my favourite anything was when I came into recovery. I'd be what anyone needed me to be, or what would get the best reaction. But I realised in early recovery that my favourite colour was green, so I got green everything. I put up green curtains to replace the fitted sheet hung haphazardly around the rail, I got a green velvet dress and painted my nails pine.

My phone background was always a visual check-in for me in early sobriety. Sometimes it was a picture of my brother and sister, sometimes an orca, because I cannot believe they are real and I live on the same planet as them. Whatever it was, it was something I unavoidably had to see every day, so it made sense to make it something that made me smile.

I'm a horrible photographer, so I tried describing things instead: the style, the nuance of the colour and the strangeness of shapes. I became a moodboard and scrapbook person, spending evenings slicing up magazines and glueing the colours, patterns, shapes and features that got my attention.

Touch

When I'm emotionally vulnerable, I feel skinless pressing against any internal or external discomfort – the world isn't just happening to me, it's assaulting me.

When everything feels spiky on the inside, running my hands over the smoothness of a polished stone balances it. When I want to tear my skin off, covering it in my softest clothing can dampen that urge. When I feel I'm buzzing with nerves from the inside out, smoothing moisturiser over myself softens that in every way. Touching myself with care is a small but significant thing that makes a world of difference for me.

In the realm of other people's touch, you get to honour your physical boundaries in recovery, and be mindful of who you let in your physical space. Even if you are flinchy around touch, like I can be, anyone can become touch starved. In sobriety we can experience the intimate comfort of non-sexual touch, with massages, being tactile with friends or holding hands saying the serenity prayer. If those aren't available, there is always the warm embrace of a weighted blanket, a bath and a cup of tea.

Make your celebration of your senses a daily devotion to gradually build each day, to experience the world in a way that doesn't hurt. It isn't dependent on restriction or excess. It's acknowledging what is there, and perhaps putting in place some grounding touchstones for when things get too much.

V. Emotions

Being healed isn't about feeling nothing. Being healed is about feeling the appropriate emotions at the appropriate times and still being able to come back to yourself. That's just life.
— Stephanie Foo, *What My Bones Know: A Memoir of Healing from Complex Trauma* (2022)

When you realise you're an adult with the emotional literacy of a teenager. When feeling your feelings feels like a bit too much to handle. When you've been detached from yourself for so long, you don't even know how you feel any more.

It's 2011, I'm 19 and on a psychiatric hold, because it has been decided that I am a danger to myself. The world is ending, and no one seems to notice; they're just wheeling me carefully down a corridor. Darkness is spilling into the whole universe — and they're talking normally, one of them laughs and I think they're making fun of me. I want to breathe fire, scream, but there's a gnarled knot in my throat, pumping and pouring shadows onto everything in my sight. Maybe I'd never sing again. There are children's drawings on the wall. I can hear the hairs on people's arms move. In the ward there's a rustle in the corner, someone leaning from their bed to get something from a plastic bag. It keeps happening. If it keeps happening, I will never sleep, and that panics me. I wonder if I could take out the greasy needle attached to a drip and run. My arms won't move, so I resign myself to the bed and wish I had my phone. The rustle persists. In my head the ward looks like a VAD hospital in the First World War, and we are in some derelict stately home with a hundred beds spread out from wall to wall. My imagination saves me from reality, then the rustle.

'Shut the fuck up,' I say it into the darkness. There is a sigh, and it stops for the night.

Thinking there are at least a hundred of us in the ward, I hope my late-night seething will be anonymised. There are just four of us, and I have the double misfortune of being not only in the psych ward, but the least popular girl there. The woman next to me spends the whole first day convincing me that the deep parallel gashes on her wrists and forearm, held together with medical tape, are from a new medical procedure they're trying out to check her blood pressure. Another silently applies layer over layer of make-up all day. I decide to sit in my bed and learn music for my upcoming competitions, and talk excitedly to the nurses about how I am going to sing at the Met. They won't stop asking me about the scars on my arms and why I tried to kill myself, and I tell them I wasn't trying to kill myself. I just had a bad day, the darkness got a bit much, but now I have to prepare for my upcoming German Lieder class. In a gown (hospital, not ball), I practise the pronunciation and diligently analyse harmony, as if I am in the library with my classmates.

A doctor, a woman in her early thirties in a neat, floral, knee-length dress, tells me that if I don't stop drinking, my life expectancy might be as low as 25. I'm not as fazed by this as I thought I would be. The darkness will have me one day, and that's just how it will be. I feel too much to stop drinking. If you felt things the way I did, you would drink like me, too.

Some friends come to visit me, Sarah greeting me with 'You are a fucking idiot' and handfuls of the real-life magazines I love. We sit together for the hour, reading *Love it* and *Take a Break*. Sarah asks me what happens now, and I tell her I need to perform 'Seligkeit' in my Lieder performance class on Wednesday. She looks at me knowing I know that's not what she meant, but I'm not going to say anything else on the matter.

My drip was finally taken out, a psychiatrist evaluated me, saying they would be in touch for a follow-up, and I stood outside the ward not knowing what planet I was on or what to do. I lost the pamphlets I was sent away with somewhere between the off-licence and home, then gave a terrible performance of 'Seligkeit' in my German Lieder class, sounding like I'd just got out of hospital for a suicide attempt I wouldn't admit to. I tried to get sober shortly after, a serious and fearful attempt that lasted six months. I never did get the follow-up; perhaps it was in the pile of unopened letters I kept in the bin bag by my door, or maybe I ignored the call. I never wanted to face the embarrassment of going back to the psych ward. I committed to either holding myself together better next time, or, if the darkness was to ever take me again, I would do a better job of ending it. Except I didn't, and I returned a year later after a boyfriend whose name

I don't even remember blocked me during an argument, and I couldn't think of anything to do other than overdose. No one came to visit me this time, and I didn't blame them.

Eventually having my realisation that something inside me wanted to live, and I either had to change or die, at age 25 felt oddly significant. The life that I was living did, in fact, reach its maximum expectancy, and I needed to start a new one. One of the reasons I drank was because I was pathologically obsessed with changing how I felt. One of the conditions of this new life was that I had to learn to feel things, without literally trying to kill myself or drinking myself into a coma.

Some things I feel:
I feel a constant need to be guilty about something I haven't done.
I hate how soft I am sometimes. When you give a fuck, you feel like you have something to lose. I also love how soft I am – I get so much out of the little things.
I am scared that I have a limited amount of happiness and I can't spend too much, so sometimes sadness feels like a relief.
I honestly believe my parents did a good job, and I hate that I didn't appreciate them at the time.
I am so fucking sad sometimes, even when it doesn't make sense.
I am sometimes so amazed by the fact that I'm alive that I do a little dance when I'm waiting at traffic lights.

They come and go, each with their varying level of intensity, bouncing off my experiences with the world around me.

Sometimes they are trains that I don't board, sometimes they take me to a station I stay at for a while, sometimes they tug and sometimes they drag.

But in my first year of sobriety, my feelings felt like a threat to my sanity. An emotion could ruin an entire day. I flipped through them rapidly, getting whiplash when they appeared out of nowhere – luring me into them with the threat of an eternity in their jaws. They felt inappropriate. When I was supposed to be happy I felt hollow. When I was meant to be sad I couldn't stop laughing.

I didn't have words for them, so they turned into grabby wantings: I want to feel OK, I want out of this, I want to masturbate all day, I want to drink, I want to emigrate to Japan, I want to rob a bank, I want to kill myself.

I thought that these were examples of feelings, when really they were frantic escapist desires ricocheting off feelings I couldn't tolerate. 'I want to feel OK' meant I felt uneasy or threatened; 'I want out of this' meant I felt trapped; 'I want to masturbate all day' meant I felt lonely; 'I want to emigrate to Japan' meant I felt bored; 'I want to rob a bank' meant I felt insecure; 'I want to kill myself' meant I felt overwhelmed and 'I want to drink' meant I felt literally anything.

There was no template for how I experienced my emotions; I had a loop of 'feel, panic, react'. Or 'feel, panic, surrender to the fact that I was a broken individual, destined to be permanently maladjusted to life'. It felt like I needed to start the fight, harm myself, numb out, listen to the hateful internal monologue, close the blinds and lie in this feeling for a season.

My earliest feeling is looking at myself in the bathroom mirror before PE in primary school, feeling disgust at the lonely, ugly girl in the red polo shirt and shorts. At night I stared blankly, thinking about how much I wanted to go home, in the only bedroom I'd ever had. This feeling persisted no matter how much I pushed up against it, covered my walls with chopped-up magazine scraps of all things that felt like 'me' or tried to appease it by pretending to like what other people liked.

Then came a great release, I became a 12-year-old goth discovering poetry, grunge music and 2000s Tumblr. With some nostalgia, I remember this era as almost euphoric. I stopped being a bag of nerves who only wanted to play the piano well in the hope someone would tell me I was good, and became someone who spoke in hyperbolic song lyrics, doodled pictures of fallen angels in my jotters and wore ripped fishnets on purpose to unconsciously signal, 'I am done doing my best, have me at my worst.'

I was confused, angry and anxious but had given myself permission to be sad about it, scream, write and make music about it for no other reason than the act of doing it. I wasn't alone; I belonged with people who felt and expressed themselves in the same way – even if it was just hanging out by the Morrisons fire exit at the weekend, or going to gigs in community centres, singing about things we didn't understand yet and how one day we'd leave this shitty town.

My feelings were so rapturous they couldn't be unfelt. My first crush felt like the greatest love story ever told – their name ran along every sheet of paper my pen touched to make this incredible revelation of what a heart can do feel more real. When I heard a song I liked it was the best song ever – I wanted it in my veins. My first heartbreak was the most catastrophic thing to ever happen, so I wrote poems and songs about it, without judging, censoring or comparing myself (unless reading my own work and saying, 'Yes, I am the Sylvia Plath of my generation'). Having my independence questioned told me what I did and didn't want. I developed rage and ideals. I felt things, for better or for worse, and I accepted their presence.

Of course there is some retention bias here. We are more prone to remember the good feelings around this period, because if we were to carry every feeling from adolescence it would be too much to handle.

That window of unapologetic, unselfconscious feeling gets shut, sometimes quickly

I didn't grow up feeling beautiful; I grew up pale, thin and unremarkable, praying earnestly in church on Sundays for my boobs to start growing, and googling plastic surgery on the family computer. But older boys started to take an interest in me, and it made me feel less plain. The boys my own age thought I was weird, and I let them, because I would rather reject them than be rejected, I thought I was cooler than them anyway, edgier and more interesting. I thought I was older than I was, and could handle what that meant. Drinking cans in a forest near the edge of town, I remember one of the senior boys telling me I was beautiful, and wanting to believe him. I remember his fingers moving against the fabric outside my underwear, to inside, wondering why someone would do that and how much it hurt. I remember him telling me to enjoy it, and wondering, *Am I supposed to be enjoying this?* I distracted myself by counting the number of leaves on each branch above us. It was at home afterwards when I realised that what we did was probably sex and I didn't think this was how it would happen for me. I didn't cry, not even in the bathroom, finding dirt and bark between my thighs, from where I was pressed up against the tree.

It felt like something I couldn't write, scream, sing or even tell anyone about. I felt like a scared child again, not even entitled to how I was feeling, because what was there to feel anyway? I wasn't injured, it wasn't violent. It was just something that happened, but something that filled me with something distressing I couldn't quite understand. This, and the way my tutor was starting to look at me, solidified the belief that I was built to be used, in a way that beautiful, sweet, unbroken girls aren't. I would never see my body in quite the same way again, knowing how other people saw it, and what they would do to it.

It felt like my cue to grow up. I started to take singing more seriously. I developed the muscles for embarrassment and judgement and started to get my sense of self from what other people thought of me. We stopped being goths and got on with our lives and responsibilities. Our school wasn't one with a lot of resources or opportunities flowing from it, so if we wanted something, we had to work hard. At home I withdrew, shutting my parents and siblings out, distancing myself into my own head where I thought I would be safe and they would be spared from the inconvenience of my existence. I realised that what other people called an eating disorder gave me a sense of order. I discovered what self-injury was and what it could do for me.

The window of feeling shut, and my emotions remained suffocatingly inside – the days of expression were over, and never having learned to process or cope with my emotions, I thought I needed to sacrifice them to move on, which also meant sacrificing wonder, passion and optimism. I substituted feeling my emotions for performing them. Singing was a socially acceptable scream, and people love an elemental woman on the edge of a breakdown on-stage. My feelings weren't a feral animal that terrified people there; they were something important, artistic and worthy of praise. I found alcohol, and for a while it gave me the only feeling I could tolerate – one I felt was my choice.

What doesn't kill you makes you pretty averse to feeling your feelings

Like your teenage self, feelings can be this embarrassing thing that you don't have time for and can't admit to – like the books you used to like and the films you built your personality around as an adolescent. Sadness is your *Fight Club*; anger is your *Girl, Interrupted*; enjoyment over something simple is whatever wizard or vampire you had your first sex dream about. Mortifying. If we do talk about our feelings, we preface it with an apology or an acknowledgement that they 'probably will think it's stupid but' – and then say one of the most devastating things imaginable. We can also feel the need to suppress feelings for safety, as expressing how you feel might put relationships at risk or provoke retaliation. They might feel pointless. You can't tell someone whose punch is inching closer from the wall to your face how you feel. You can't tell your boss how you feel, as they remind you how replaceable you are. You can't tell your landlord who raised your rent how you feel. What good will it do? Tie them up, suck them down, get on with it. We're adults, we don't have time for that. A lot of parents are scared of their teenagers because they express the things they feel they're not allowed to. They're one of the most vulnerable mirrors to look into.

Drinking seemed to be the convenient avenue for expressing things that would feel inappropriate in any other context. It's not often you scream your grievances with a group of friends in a cathartic ritual, but with a few bottles of wine it's quite normal. You can tell the drunk girl in the club bathroom that men sexualised you before you even started your period, and she'll probably hug you and tell you the worst thing that ever happened to her. Indulging sadness with self-destruction helps give it a sense of grandeur and meaning – you can romanticise it; you're on an Orpheus-in-the-underworld mission down into the underbelly of your psychological depths to come back with greater wisdom, rather than just rotting in bed waiting for your flatmates to leave so you can use the kitchen by yourself. A night of blackout is a break from yourself, and no one thinks you're weird for abandoning your consciousness when you do it with a group of people.

If a feeling is big enough to drink on, it matters. It's an adult emotion, not an embarrassing or trivial one. 'I need a drink' is a socially acceptable way of saying 'I'm unhappy' and no one questions it.

When you put the drink down, you meet the teenager that picked it up. Past the point of physical withdrawal, sobriety is basically how well you deal with getting your feelings back, and what you do with that.

No feeling is forbidden, but we have to get literate with them if we are going to live with them and reach an appropriate level of maturity for the life we want to live. We can sometimes have an aversion to adulthood and a resentment that a lot of our childhoods were cut short. We can't play out our emotional life as adolescents do, because we are no longer adolescents, however meeting our teenage selves can be an entry point for how it is to honestly feel something, and see how we can deal with it, as adults. We can give ourselves the gift of what we lost when life happened – validation, patience and acceptance. We can fill in the parts we missed the first time around and process our emotions safely and compassionately, finding what is underneath them and looking for the safety we may not have had before. We can do so without culling our emotional lives.

I was too sad to realise I was livid

There can be a sick satisfaction in being really sad. When our sadness has taken everything from us, no one can take away the fact that we are sad. Not just in the self-aware, cynical and terminally online way, but in a way that shocks, scares and appals people – in a way that stops washing, wants to smoke in the bath and can't drink water because nothing else fits inside right now. I felt like my sadness gave me depth and made me interesting, so I fetishised it, made it part of my identity, because I couldn't imagine being anything else.

Sadness is an inevitable and natural symptom of being human – but depression has teeth. Sadness is a variable state and often a reasonable reaction. Depression requires help. The cruel thing about depression is that it keeps itself alive by making you averse to anything that would make you feel better – the symptoms run into lack of personal care, self-sabotaging, altered eating, isolation, suicidal ideation and feeling like a dusty skeleton going through the motions of things you used to enjoy. Then there's the trip switch that flips from feeling the entirety of the world's suffering to nothing at all; all you care about is when you get to eat next, and you imagine an invigilator watching your nap schedule, ready to tell you you're a bad adult. You feel like a dead lightbulb, with nothing to give, even if the light switch has been flicked on. You can look into the eyes of people you have long histories with and think, *Who are you?* Then, a return to despair, rumination and a quicker death seeming like the most realistic way of ending the thudding ache of this collapsed hive of a brain. Acknowledging and accepting the reality of your situation, rather than ignoring or romanticising it, can give you agency to decide what to do with it, and seek clarity whether you are sad, depressed or both.

As I moved through my depression, I realised its despair was sometimes masking a rage I didn't feel entitled to. A lot of us feel like we aren't angry people. Sometimes drink would wear away the dam holding my anger, sending my rage spitting out of me. I would be so disgusted with myself and my potential to hurt someone, I would make a conscious effort to control my temper rather than losing it. So many of us live in fear of angry people, flinching at sudden movements, skin pricking at a raised voice, feeling a flush of heat when a fist hits a table or a resonant voice reminds us that rage is under the skin of anyone we meet and it might come for us. When your emotional world erupts out of you in anger you get less sympathy, and I at least wanted some pity if I wasn't going to be happy.

Many of us thaw out and realise we've been angry this whole time. We turned our anger inwards, and it seethed under the sadness, the apathy and the exhaustion as a long and slow self-loathing. It might feel less ruthless than being at the mercy of rage, because we can argue it isn't hurting anyone. The cost of that is forgetting that we are someone who is hurting.

My anger was not like fire, it was acid. It was usually quiet, often unnoticed, and it silently destroyed me from the inside. Many women are realising that their sadness was anger, and perhaps some of their anger was sadness, all along. Either way, anger felt like a forbidden thing, which carried all the complications that forbidden things do.

I got sober, and got angry.

The sense of sorrow I felt when I thought about my past turned into fury. I wanted vengeance over peace. I watched 'good-for-her' movies, like *Midsommar, Gone Girl, Carrie, Heathers* — where the protagonist overcomes with revenge and violence rather than acceptance and grace. I challenged people when they said that the greatest revenge is that people who were cruel to you have to live with themselves, and I have a life well lived, seething, 'How is that revenge? They're fine, and I have to do this colossal amount of work just to feel OK?'

Feeling anger is not a moral failing. There are a lot of things to be angry about. Anger precipitates change. It could have saved us when it was the current that pushed 'no' through the fear. It can be the last residue of energy that moves us, that gets us punching out of bed, even if we're doing it out of spite. Anger feels like a shield, a taste of wrath to protect us from despair. It's protective when we don't have an internal system that can identify mistreatment yet. Anger is the cry of 'I am human'. It is immediate and has velocity; it feels like it has somewhere to go. It sometimes feels like the only thing to believe in.

But anger can want to tear into things and have something to blame. It can imprint itself on the people we love the most and those who deserve it the least when it finds no other target. Anger is natural, but we can't pitch a tent there.

Anger is a messenger, telling us we are experiencing something outside of what we can tolerate, and that we must listen. Anger can build, stack and get stuck, but it can also be given words, be expressed in a safe place, be given an outlet, be given a thread, to see if it weaves through into a pattern. It can be put together with a bigger picture and point us in the direction of where change has to be made – in us, our circumstances or the world.

Rage is the call to pause, not to make decisions or judgements. It is the point between acceptance and action, where we can choose not to act in rage. If our anger is the only thing keeping us safe, we need to find genuine safety, and compassionate connection if we are burning alive. We must hear what anger is telling us, tend to what needs to be tended, say what needs to be said and make an effort to change what needs to be changed.

We might also not be angry for the reason we think we are, and just because we acknowledge we are angry doesn't mean we are right. We might also just be hungry.

Let the soft animal of your body feel your stupid feelings

Sometimes we're emotionally exhausted and our brain has no idea what to do with itself. Sometimes we numb out on purpose, and sometimes we're just numb, rolling between different anti-depressants trying to find 'the one', when in reality we also need a liveable wage, affordable housing and more helpful conditions to manage what we are dealing with. Sometimes it can all be so confusing to be a feeling creature, like you're defective for feeling so much, and sometimes so little. Our feelings aren't inconvenient imperfections – we *should* be feeling things. It's not a personal failure to be angry or distressed when responding to things that are infuriating or distressing, or to feel lonely, stressed or overwhelmed in a world that can be lonely, stressful and overwhelming.

Living with our emotions isn't about jamming the one we want into our brain, or expecting to feel unwaveringly the one we think we 'should' be having. Emotions are flexible, and the more experience we get with them, the better acquainted we get with a centre to return to. We learn to accept and adapt, feel what we feel, for as long as we need to, and continue in the way that lines up with what we want to express in the moment.

When you're healing, sadness, anger and numbness can make you feel like a fraud, like all of this work is for nothing. The reality is, people in recovery feel everything that a person feels. Healing isn't a quest to feel happy all the time that we're failing until we have achieved that. Our feelings don't have to be pathologised away. The goal isn't to manage our emotions like an Olympic sport until we can fully control them. Healing means feeling everything and having the strength to carry it, maybe even being enlivened by it. We usually cannot control the reality of our first feeling, which is why we must gain tools for rage, skills for depression, opposite-actions for our self-destructive impulses and safety barriers for the urgent reaches for security when we fear abandonment or rejection.

There is no life free of emotion. Experiencing our emotions is the first step to managing them – we can't skip that first part, and we don't want to get too obsessed with the second. Emotions are feelings in motion, and they will always be on the move. Feelings don't pass into nothing; they pass into the next feeling. For them to move, so must I.

The worst thing about sobriety is getting your feelings back. It's also the best thing

As someone who has felt their feelings so strongly it felt like a threat to their life, I preface this section by encouraging my siblings in suicidal ideation to get whatever protection and support you need alongside these principles.

Our emotions contain information that we need in order to proceed in a way that lines up with what matters to us and who we actually are. They can be rabid fireflies, showing us in fragmented ways something internal, which is down a dark path but that needs to be seen. It seems like such a scam sometimes, that what I am feeling is simply what I'm feeling, but I can have greater acceptance of my life when I accept how I feel about it. A lot of the pain and exhaustion of being a deeply feeling person came from fighting the feeling itself, and a lot of the pain in my life comes from the consequences of acting on the feeling before taking a pause.

Many of us haven't felt a feeling from start to finish. The muscle to follow an emotion through and sustain it may have atrophied, so we need to practise.

Feel, pause, breathe, act.

In a safe environment, ask yourself how you are doing. Breathe around it, letting whatever comes up simply come up. You can slam your face into a pillow, tear up tiny bits of paper, scribble in a notebook – but try to stay in an observational, non-judgemental space where you can respond, rather than immediately react.

Responding rather than reacting, simply observing it curiously, can create a dialogue that doesn't have hatred and danger attached to it. With more practice, you can recognise emotions more quickly, and they start to feel less like a foreign language. Consistency means that eventually, rather than needing to set time aside to feel how you are feeling, you can do it as you go, in the moment.

Writer Geneen Roth explains a technique of describing the feeling by using colour, shape, texture, speed and its position in the body in her book *Women Food and God*. I realised that anger was stuck spinning as a red ball in my throat, shame was a frozen pit in my stomach and love was a green velvet blanket over my chest.

If you don't have words, you can simply take the first step of accepting that you are feeling deeply right now and make space for it, whatever that feeling might be. This opens us up to having space for emotions we may enjoy, or ones that feel enriching. You don't have to be happy about how you're feeling. You can set a timer for five minutes, and write about how fucking shit everything is. Expressing your feelings somewhere you don't have to censor yourself helps get the wildest possible thoughts out, tangled, exposed, messy. When I do this I can then share it with someone to defang it, and see any perspectives I've missed – my blind spots. I can put it into a bigger context and maybe even laugh about it. My feelings might be valid, but they're often quite insane.

Audre Lorde says in *A Burst of Light* (1988), 'Feelings are not wrong but you are accountable for the behaviour you use to satisfy those feelings.' As much as we must honour the reality of our feelings and how real they feel to us, we are the only person who is responsible for our actions. Rather than indulge in a feeling with a drastic action or use it as a justification to engage in something we might regret, we can acknowledge our reaction, accept it as ours and act in a way that lines up with our values and not at anyone else's expense.

You clear the way to the next right action when you check in with yourself. You might need to slow down or have a fire put under you. You might need to be taken for a walk, be lost in another universe of a book or a film, have a hard phone call, reassess some things or apologise. You might need help with something, to move your body, get engaged with something bigger than you or have some fun. If you are empty, you can offer up this emptiness to something loving to be filled. You can have arms around you, even when you can't feel them, or light a candle, which doesn't change anything but at least the room smells nice now. Sometimes you can connect, meditate, wash the mugs in the sink, make someone a cup of coffee, and still feel sad, but at least you've done something that points you in a direction away from being taken under. Things are less likely to change if you're pretending the feeling isn't there or solely fixating on how terrible you feel, and how terrible you are for feeling that way.

Not all our emotions will be proportional, because some of them are rooted in something more painful than we fully understand at the moment. In these situations, we can use a quick DBT skill called 'Check the Facts'. In the pause we can assess what evidence we have, so we can separate the emotion from the events. The more we map our emotions, the less we let them drag us into reactions to something that happened years ago. We can separate the interpretations and assumptions, contextualise and respond less reactively.

When we feel ourselves getting obsessed with our feelings, we can get out of our own heads by asking someone about their life or doing something for someone. It's hard to think about yourself too much when you're earnestly and consciously thinking about someone else. I can sit all day thinking about my feelings, or I can take a shower, meditate, call a friend and be there. Sharing our pain with each other, with the intention of getting through it together, is the most loving act there is.

Sometimes we have to commit to acting better than we feel, and we can do that without denying how we feel. Recovery means I can follow the plan, and not my mood, and see if that makes me feel better. We can accept that we feel like shit, and acknowledge that this is the life we fought for, and the very least we can do is show up.

Time takes time

Sometimes I want to believe that an intellectual understanding of something will transfer into a seamless application, with immediate results. It would make sense that the harder we think about it, the more we can master it. Sometimes perfectionism bleeds into the pursuit of wholeness. You can get a bit of traction in one area, and fixate on the next thing, developing an obsession with perfect healing – anything less and you must be doing something wrong. Not every second is supposed to be spent on self-betterment – we don't want our life to be a constant rumination on what we think is broken about us. The time it takes to process these things is part of the process. The fact that we have the language of healing as such an available option when generations before did not is incredible. Here we can combine the assets of the old principle of 'getting on with it', and the modern wisdom of 'feeling your feelings', into 'feel your feelings, so you can proceed accordingly'. Time takes time, and the more we learn, the easier it gets.

Here is a fact that blew my mind: not a single feeling, good or bad, will last forever

Robert Plutchik, the psychologist most famous for inventing the 'feelings wheel', theorised that humans are capable of 34,000 unique emotions. Most of us are fixated on 'happy'. So much of what we do, buy and aspire towards is a reach for happiness – we've druggified the very nature of happiness; we mainline 'dopamine hits' from our behaviours.

But all this work makes you really big inside. If you've been to the darkest parts of your mind and steer easily into melancholy, balanced on the other end is a tremendous and just as sensitive capacity for gratitude and love. You must give life-breath to the currents of joy, playfulness and patience so they aren't consumed. They must be given the same current as the devastation, pain and fear we have been so tormented by before. They all exist in the container of the universe inside us. The magnitude of our feelings doesn't always have to be burdensome – music, art, drama, poetry, stories and philosophy move us in a way that matches the parameters of our depth and width of feeling, in ways that feel miraculous. Our empathy, sensitivity and tenderness can be an asset to those around us – they can be the thing that someone needs to feel seen, safe or represented. We, the kids who felt things deeply, have a passion that can be directed and rendered useful, powerful and impactful. With time, we fill out the edges. We can align our emotions to our desires. They stop being wants and urges that grab at us, and they become efforts and processes that make up a meaty middle of life that is so spacious, yet so full.

The act of emotional honesty that creates intimacy with others, by saying what we mean and meaning what we say, can start with the (not-always-simple) simple acknowledgement of how we feel within ourselves. Our feelings may have been belittled or weaponised against us. They may have made us antisocial and confusing. They may have made us really shit to be around at parties. But I have never hated myself into changing the way I feel (actually, I have hated my way into feeling much worse).

The more space you have inside, the more capability you have to live not just in the black and white of your feelings. There is a tiny part of sadness in every joy; there is a small joy in every sadness. You can be grateful, as well as a little bit frightened; pissed off, as well as excited for something. You don't have to gather everything up and make it into one unified feeling that fits somewhere on a scale – you learn resilience to carry the universe inside you. That's what peace feels like.

When we experience our emotions rather than have them entirely dictate our behaviour, we are met with facts about ourselves – and even they are allowed to change. That's not instability but a natural flux of experiencing what it is to be human. We are not static. Part of growing is changing, and letting ourselves be changed. You are not broken. There is no permanent state of bad or good because there are no permanent states. But there is what you are dealing with today, then there is the choice of what you do with it. Feelings are big, but they're just a small part of something bigger: who you are.

You are alive. Feel everything.

Let everything happen to you: beauty and terror.
Just keep going. No feeling is final.
– 'Go to the Limits of Your Longing',
Rainer Maria Rilke (1905)

VI. Escapism

Behaviours can bring their own highs, but the purpose of the high is not necessarily pleasure in the experience, it's everything it blots out.
— Octavia Bright, *This Ragged Grace* (2023)

When you stop drinking and realise you're a sex, food, relationship, television, nicotine, adrenalin, fantasy and shopping addict. When the one thing you cannot tolerate is the present moment. When the void calls, and you will look for anything to fill it.

When I was 23 and trying to launch as a young artist for the 2017 season, I secured an audition in Philadelphia that would get me in the room with people who held the keys to my career. After months of preparation, and hundreds of dollars spent on travel and a hotel, I sent my friends a hopeful dressing-room picture, walked confidently onto the stage – and completely bombed. It hadn't been a good season. A career in opera means getting about 10 per cent of the jobs you audition for, if you're lucky, and I was tired of being strong, tired of waiting for the big break that would make me feel complete. I tearfully walked down Locust Street, found a bar, got into a car and woke up in a room full of guns, thinking, *How the fuck did I get here?* I was in a foreign city, lying next to a stranger and a weapon that could kill me – but at least I didn't just feel like a failed opera singer any more. I wasn't in my body, I wasn't me. I didn't have to focus on my disappointment, I had to find my way back to my hotel and the next thing that was going to distract me, and a few days later I was a plus one at a Greek wedding with a man I had met on Tinder.

When your feelings are unacceptable to you, learning that you can drink, sniff, fuck, text, buy or light something between the onset of an emotion and the point where it becomes uncomfortable feels like the perfect escape.

Aside from the perpetual truth of 'I don't like feeling things', my need to escape is deeply connected to the hole in my soul that lies under my addiction. This lonely, anxious, empty space takes the shape of whatever I think will make me feel whole. This hungry chasm's presence tells me I must seek that thing, behaviour or activity, because I am unable to tolerate being alive without what it wants to be fed. It's uncomfortable to exist with this ragged tear and the void underneath it, but fulfilling its desires by satisfying its cravings creates a need for more, because it is a shapeshifter. It morphed into a million different 'I needs', and kept me running, looking for the next thing that might make me feel OK.

Under my addiction is a deep need to escape not only my feelings, but myself, my circumstances and the reality of this void. It's interesting to me that we use the term 'fix' for our drug or high of choice – between desiring and obtaining it, there is the belief that it will fix what is broken and fill this hole. Alcohol and drugs once unburdened me of my sense of incompleteness, loneliness and alienation, which seemed to have been with me from birth; it replaced the emptiness with warmth. In them I could dissolve, evaporate and disappear.

The roots of addiction run deep and plant themselves in this hole. When we stop doing the thing that is killing us quickest, other things take its place. Recovery isn't just about stopping doing things; it is about treating the cause of our desire to use them.

When I got sober, drinking and drugs ceased being the escape route from my feelings, so the behaviours that predated my drinking reappeared – the things I had before alcohol was an answer to the question of me. I lunged for them, running for the present moment's exit sign. If I felt unattractive, I could suck desire out of another person; if I felt empty, I could binge eat; if I was overwhelmed, I could enter the lives of others with eight hours of TV and deep dives on my ex's ex on social media.

Being present for everything you feel, alongside the entire human experience, is challenging – especially if you don't enjoy the experience of being human, especially when you're sober. I felt claustrophobic, as if I was in an underground cave, cornered, softly crying as someone tried to explain high-school maths to me – when in reality I was just having to act like someone who opened their post, answered their emails and occasionally didn't get their way. Realising that I was unavoidably an adult with adult responsibilities was like waking up in a stranger's bed, not knowing what happened or how I was going to get out of it, and my inner child was somewhere in the background, absolutely livid about the entire situation. Additionally, real life bored me – I sought intensity, hyperbole, chosen pain and a narrative arc.

When we learned about Wagner in musicology, the lecturer explained that the dense harmonies, four hours of plot and thousands of years of history could be simplified down to 'tension and release' – from the unexpected pull of the Tristan chord, to Brünnhilde's immolation, to Isolde's ascension. It suited the characters I played on-stage, and my life once the orchestra had packed up. There was the tension (of getting a council tax bill I didn't understand and my brain's leitmotif of 'stupid, stupid, you're stupid') and the release of throwing myself into anything to help take the edge off, even if it burned me alive (or didn't text me back).

A day in the life of an escape artist

I thought by a year sober I would be famous, thin, married and a property owner. It felt like a fair deal: I get sober, and then get given everything I want. A year turned over in 2019, and though I had gone 365 days without drinking or doing drugs, I was still Lauren McQuistin, and something about that devastated me. People hugged me, gave me cards, told me I was a miracle, and I cried in Dominic's car as he drove me home from work, embarrassed to tell him, because I felt like so little had changed. I ran my fingers under my eyes, trying to catch the mascara running down my cheeks, and sniffed, 'I don't know, I just thought it would feel different.'

I shared this with my sponsor, expecting to be told that it was something uniquely terrible and specific to me. She told me it was natural – I put an unrealistic expectation on the day, and now I was disappointed. She said it simply and without hesitation, as if it was the most obvious thing in the world, which maybe it was. I had put an expectation on sobriety, and was now realising it isn't a genie that grants your wishes, it's a method to get your shit together. I was still Lauren McQuistin, and the point was continuing to learn to live with that. I had forgotten that a year ago I wanted to die, and now I did not. In fact, there was a light behind my eyes that I don't think I'd ever had.

Later that year, at almost eighteen months sober, I was freshly graduated from Yale and feeling slightly impotent as work continued to be challenging to come by, as it was for everyone in the industry at that age and stage. In response, I was ordering $50 worth of smoked meats from Bear's Smokehouse Barbecue making elaborate meal and exercise plans down to the calorie, smoking and lying about it when people said, 'Wait, aren't opera singers not supposed to do that?' and fantasising that the person who winked at me on the Subway found me, proposed by a lake, and freed me from this painful liminal space of knowing I can't be drunk, and might not always enjoy being sober.

To supplement my income, I got a job as a classical-music tour manager and was fired a month later, simply because I had no idea what I was doing, having no experience as a tour manager. I had never lost a job because of my drinking, but now I'd lost one sober. Getting on the Metro-North to New York every weekend for auditions and competitions was exhausting me, and I hadn't connected to my friends in a long time, until one came over unannounced. She found me studying German (because what if I end up moving to Germany and I don't speak German perfectly? Everyone will make fun of me), organising my side-jobs (because if I don't do the absolute most I will fall into destitution) and cleaning my flat (if I have a good living environment, I can work harder and better).

After tolerating only having half of my attention for a while, she asked, 'Can you stop cleaning the windows and tell me what's going on?'

I didn't want to. I wanted to stay busy, because if I stopped being busy, I'd have to think about what was going on. I started to perform *The Lauren Show* for my friend – tears are for the dressing room; smiles are for the stage. I hadn't cried in weeks.

My friend asked me how my sobriety was going, and I remembered all the skills I'd been taught about feeling my feelings, and how it's my honesty that will save me.

I told her it was hard right now. I was undeniably here, and kept blasting myself out of the airlock of life, because I didn't always want to be. I didn't want to drink, but it was all so uncomfortable. I should be doing better by now. I dug through my pockets to see if there was anything I could smoke, chew or swallow. She just listened, and I started to cry. After a while I felt some space inside, the discomfort loosened and I had experienced myself without completely throwing my consciousness into the sea. We talked for another hour, about our families, auditions we had coming up and how much we really hated *The Magic Flute*.

We don't always talk about self-injury in recovery so I'm going to

After flipping through enough escapism behaviours (nicotine, TV, exercising, shopping, dating, food, etc.), you can find one that scares you enough to make you realise you need to step down from doing two shows a night and a matinee as an escape artist, so you don't do it until you drown. I realised this when I recognised the return of my desire to cut.

Escapism behaviours are pain management. They distract us from the inevitable pain of being alive and the fear of any potential pain. Sometimes the behaviours are a chosen pain, one that feels like our choice.

When I was 11, I realised that if I hit my wrist against my hip bone it made me feel slightly better. I later read *Girl, Interrupted*, and when Susanna Kaysen described the same thing as 'wrist bashing' I was slightly surprised, because I thought I'd invented it. At 13, I graduated to razors, and wearing long sleeves in summer.

Self-injury is one of the most loaded areas of pain management. People sometimes ask about my scars, and after I tell them it was a shark attack or body modification from the spirit world to grant me my powers, I say that some people might have considered getting a new haircut, but when I was facing something too painful to understand this felt like the only thing I could do in the moment. That's how dark the darkness was: the only way to appease it was to carve into my flesh. It doesn't make sense, but the darkness didn't make sense either, and I needed something bad to happen, something that felt real, to explain it. It was easier to focus on a physical wound with an obvious source, than an invisible, overwhelming force that people would tell me was all in my head, and therefore unimportant.

When alcohol stopped working my cutting accelerated. I kept a razor behind my phone case to use before rejoining the party, having let some air out of the tyre. There was a relief in deciding to cut myself, knowing that what I was feeling would change soon. It only started to hurt when the wave of emotional pain subsided and I realised what I'd done, but at the time it felt as normal as taking a paracetamol. I want to say it was bloodletting or my form of transcendental meditation, that I was following medieval rituals or had some poetic reason. Maybe I was trying to punish myself subconsciously, but in the moment it didn't feel like a punishment, it felt practical.

The National Institute for Health and Care Excellence (NICE) reports that around one in every four 16- to 24-year-old women (25.7 per cent) reported having self-harmed at some point.[1] There are many of us with the same white and pink puffy canyons crossing our arms and thighs, juxtaposed against summer dresses and business attire – done when language about these behaviours wasn't as widespread. The outsiders hadn't inherited the Earth by way of the internet and tagged public communities, apart from the 'To Write Love on Her Arms' Myspace page. It's written off as teenage behaviour, something melodramatic. It's infantilised – just immature girls seeking attention. It's easier to belittle the feelings of people in so much pain that they are driven to temporary relief that causes permanent damage than to acknowledge it. It's easier to ignore it than to be terrified by it. But it should be terrifying. It is terrifying that people feel that support is so unavailable that self-injury feels rational. It's uncomfortable; people don't like to see pain and its effects made physical. It's easier to watch it be numbed out in the pub, or in achievement and acquiring things.

I will always have a sense of kinship with people who have visible scars. We know what it's like to have them be such an undeniable part of ourselves that we forget they're there, and are only reminded when we notice someone noticing, their eyes not quite sure what to do. We know that unique spike of anxiety when you meet someone new and your body tells a story you aren't ready to tell yet, or there's a camera around and you're in short sleeves. My scars are as healed as they will ever be and they still rise at different heights, their topography erratic. When my skin goes pink with warmth they will always be pale flashes of the past. Scar tissue never fully regains the strength and flexibility of skin, but that doesn't stop it from being miraculous in its own right. My body healed in the way it knew how, and though I am forever altered, the patchwork of my arms and thighs tells me that I made it out somehow. As much as they are a reminder of a level of pain I can't even identify with any more, they are also a reminder of my survival, and the opportunity to heal.

A few weeks after my friend's visit I was in another 'so-close,-but-not-today' moment of my career, when I placed just under the winner's bracket in a competition in Kansas City. It was the second time I had won the district and advanced to regionals, but not quite reaching the final, on the Metropolitan Opera stage – my dream since childhood. I had the options of busying myself with my flight back to New Haven, feedback and emails, or escaping reality by pretending to be really, really OK with it and engaging with four or five behaviours to displace the heaviness in my chest. I did the secret third thing. I sat on the floor of a bathroom in the theatre, did some grounding exercises, cried, called a friend and wrote my feelings out. It was about fifteen minutes of my life, and it set me free from living that moment over and over again in a way that would devastate me for years to come. It didn't stop hurting immediately, but it passed. My body knew how to navigate it, and even though I didn't trust it, I let it. I let the painful moment go. I left it there, leaning into the disappointment, barefoot in an emerald ballgown. As ridiculous as I felt, it's still one of the less disgraceful things I've done in a public bathroom.

Sweet escapes

It can be harder to withdraw from a behaviour, as opposed to a substance. There's no exact endpoint of letting go of an old idea, no poison to pass, no metric of when to know it's done. There's no day counter for 'learning to tolerate the present moment'. Rewiring your all-consuming need for instant gratification or something that makes you forget you exist is a practice, and the nutrients of it can't be bought or quantified – simply experienced.

Food, sex, spending, distraction and exercise are all unavoidable parts of being a human, and aren't inherently bad or shameful things. Realistically, there will be times when we need to and want to use these things to change how we feel. But we need to address and assess our relationships with them if they eventually toe a line of developing into patterns that might start to control us or become physically, emotionally, spiritually or financially dangerous.

Most of us start craving sugar when we stop drinking. Our brain's reward system recognises the intoxicating effect of sugar as giving the same thrill we got from drinking; it can activate the pleasure centres of the brain in similar ways. Alcohol affects our blood-sugar levels, and the longer this fluctuation continues, the more we get used to the push and pull of the peak and the drop. It creates a craving that feels like a physical need. We can create an emotional need when we get into a cycle of feeling bad, giving the bad feelings some sugar and then feeling better. Some of us use food as emotional support because it can feel like the only love and comfort we deserve. It's an accessible, safe and contained love, where we feel like there is no risk involved.

The same applies to fantasy – the world where you are safe, or wanted. As a lonely and teased kid, I imagined boys lined up outside my window arguing with each other about who loved me the most. As I grew, I obsessed over celebrities, fictional characters, people I didn't know and anyone who treated me with the slightest bit of decency – what it would be like if we were together and things were OK. Here you have complete control: you can write the script, make the plot; you don't have to deal with the unpredictability of life or the reality you've been thrashing about to avoid. You can have the love you want, afford a deposit on a house, get revenge, win arguments. You can kill your rapist.

If we stay there too long, real life can leave us feeling cheated. Idle fantasies can turn into expectations – the mother of resentment. We find ourselves getting furious at someone for something they didn't do or say in accordance with the alternate reality we created. The parallel universe feels so real it affects our emotions and our actions towards reality. We might have fantasies around revenge, moving to a different country where no one knows our name or drafts of our eulogies. Sometimes it's just a thought, something brief and meaningless – but for those of us who can get intoxicated by dark, self-destructive fantasies, what starts as a fleeting idea when our bank card is declined can find roots and take us down.

Choosing not to drink any more was a complicated and vulnerable experience; 'Add to cart' was not

We may not be able to control our life, but we can control our wardrobe. The big problems can seem insurmountable, but we can quest to find the perfect trainers, and win. Aside from any psychological need that owning things satisfies, shopping is a dopamine hit with a tangible outcome, which doesn't give us a headache or a trip to the STI clinic. Still, the consequences affect our bank balance, credit cards and overdrafts, and many of us start shoplifting, looking for adrenalin alongside the dopamine. Losing control of our spending leads to a warped perspective of our finances and what we actually need. Shopping online to emotionally regulate is easy, and mixes with impulsivity to become one of the easiest and most socially acceptable ways to manage our emotions.

Octavia Bright in her memoir *This Ragged Grace* (2023) suggests, 'I could see that the addictive impulse and capitalism were actually very well matched. They both work to commodify things. They both drive you to think in terms of what something can do for you, or how it can change the way you feel.'

The hole in the soul is fed by the need for more, and it keeps growing no matter how we try to fill it. Not only does this slowly strip the meaning away from our life, reducing everything and everyone to a fix, but it keeps us trapped in the no-win capitalistic loop. We're constantly having the missing piece advertised to us, fast-tracked and artificial, in place of the connection, support and community we really need, or the idea that we might already be, and have, enough. It's the same delusion that if we do enough of it, or try a different variety of it, it will start to work. The LED facial smoother, caffeine vape, detox flat-tummy tea, waist-toning twisting disc and summer dresses with pockets in every colour will fix the dissatisfaction we feel in our daily lives – this time will be different. We can then treat our relationships and experiences with the same level of detached urgency with the prospect of a payoff, rather than be truly in them.

Keep working, keep searching

One of the sober women I admire most in the world is Edinburgh-based lawyer Blythe. Her approach to recovery is pragmatic yet compassionate, and she will never say, 'Same old, same old,' when you ask how she is – she will be in life-drawing classes, taking pictures of polar bears or on a beach with a pile of books. However, before she could enjoy the life recovery afforded her, she had to address how her escapism showed up in work. She says: 'I've always been busy. I worked hard, had summer jobs in restaurants, went to university and kept those jobs, then started working in a relentless industry. At first, I felt it was just the reality of the job – suck it up, get on with it. It changed in COVID. I realised work had cut me off; it blocked me from real relationships with people on a deeper level. It affected my marriage, because I just wasn't there – I was always physically, or mentally, at work. It was just like drinking – I wasn't present.'

With work we can get stuck in striving for a payoff we might never receive, and realise too late that it isn't working. Blythe kept thinking, *'Just let me get through this deal, and it will be better. After I close this, it will be calmer.* Then you realise you've been saying that for ten years. I didn't know what I was working towards.'

Like all escapist behaviours, the cost outweighs the benefits, but we get trapped. 'I earned good money, and had no time to spend it. I spent most of my money on stuff to feel better – massages, holidays – but if we didn't work relentlessly and get so burnt out we wouldn't need those things.'

The emptiness at the heart of all escapist behaviours won't be treated by more. The system that puts us in the position to seek relief isn't going to tell us there's another way if it's benefiting from our engagement with it. Believing that meeting our basic needs and creating intimacy with ourselves and others will be enough might even seem like a scary or seemingly impossible thing, so we continue to reach for the thing that we know how to do, and keep seeking the meaning we're looking for in the wrong places.

'My industry is full of Type A personalities. You don't come into law because you need to be complimented. If no one is complaining, then you're doing a good job. You miss holidays, events, milestones, and barely get a thank-you. But we are secretly all seeking validation from somewhere we can't get it.'

Does the abyss need a little treat, or will it devour me whole?

It's often called a game of Whac-A-Mole: we get rid of one behaviour and another one pops up. When I was agonising over the arcade game in my head, a friend said to me that you 'can't get too well too soon'. We can't expect ourselves to put down all of these things immediately. They are mangled up in so many past experiences, we can't expect to simply snap out of it once we have the knowledge. It's a constant work in progress. We have to deal with the shark nearest the boat, the thing that's killing us the quickest, then we have a bit of space to make our next move. We can eventually see that these moles are coming from the same source of wanting, longing and discomfort in different forms – we can keep hitting the moles, or give ourselves what we really need. We can observe them, investigate where they're coming from, and see if they pop up more slowly.

We have a sexual tension between our need for pleasure and complete oblivion, and a confusing relationship with the difference between self-soothing and self-harming. It's going to take some practice before reality feels comfortable.

In my early recovery I became emotionally dependent on Butterfingers, my favourite US candy bar. I was leaning on a chocolate-covered, melted sugar and peanut-butter crisp lattice that makes my teeth hurt just thinking about it, but at least it wasn't a bottle of warm vodka I found under my bed. On Saturdays I would walk twenty minutes to a meeting, and I would make the Butterfinger last that long, unpeeling it slowly, dissolving every particle of chocolate, then melting the insides on my tongue – it got me through some hard mornings, and took me somewhere I needed to be. But there had to be a time when I could survive without it, or at least have it as an option and not a necessity. Substance abuse and eating disorders share a bedroom, and we can even mistake hunger cues for alcohol cravings, which makes a sane and stable relationship with food even more important. As our connection to our body grows, we can develop a better dialogue of what we need, and do not need, from food.

Eating with the intention of making ourselves feel better isn't wrong, and it's important to remind ourselves, in a society where people are constantly under scrutiny for their bodies and food habits, that eating is not a moral failure. It is a requirement for a functioning body. It contains culture and memories, and is centred around moments of connection. But in the arena of wanting something from the outside to make us feel better about our insides, the simplest way to check in on ourselves and our motives is to ask ourselves directly, 'Am I enjoying this, or am I using this? Is the thrill gone and am I still chasing it? Does this behaviour lead me to purging/overspending/isolating?'

We can't, and shouldn't, eliminate food, but we can change patterns by honestly reflecting and making boundaries with ourselves – we can find our patterns and make adjustments. The same can be done with spending. Restriction isn't the opposite of escapism with food and money, and making guidelines and parameters isn't punitive, it's simply making loving choices for ourselves. They can be simple, flexible and reassessed when necessary.

For example, I know I feel better when I have three meals a day. I do not act sanely around certain foods, so I don't have them in the house. I do not diet or calorie count as that leads me into obsession. I don't eat in bed. Planning means that I am less likely to crash straight into a quick fix.

Making boundaries with fantasy can be less concrete. Fantasy could have been a lifeline in our formative years, because if we were fully aware of some of the things that were happening to us before we could handle the weight of it, it might have broken us entirely – but we are creating a world that is safe now, and reality isn't such a bad thing.

If I am losing my tether to reality, I say to myself, 'I am in fantasy. I take myself to the present with kind words.' Trying this out at first felt like pouring a glass of water on a house fire, but with a bit of practice it became a natural reflex that started to work. I was once stuck in front of the mirror, wondering if plastic surgery would get an ex-obsession to come back to me. After saying this line to myself a couple of times, I started to become more aware of my surroundings, the smell of my soap, the feel of water on my hands – and I was able to get myself away from the mirror and into my day, realising that getting plastic surgery would not convince someone to text me back.

Telling someone can reality-check my narratives, and I can realise something is a bit too much right now and needs adjusting, so that reality is a more tolerable place to be. I am still a daydreamer, and I still allow myself a little bit of fantasy reading fiction and finding belonging with people who love *Star Wars* (the first universe I actually wanted to be a part of) and anime, but all of my fantasies have a foot in reality now, so I know the way back.

Fantasy is a comfort zone, and sometimes we have to take the safe risk of getting more invested in our external world. Rather than pure fantasy, we can utilise our imagination – we're allowed to be enchanted by the world around us, and see where we can imagine better lives for ourselves. We can make it an even more positive experience by putting in action, to get closer to it in reality. Fantasy can quite simply be a symptom of boredom, so it can be a call to participate in our lives more actively.

Overworking can knock aside the precious substance of being alive with being 'busy'. Overscheduling can lead to overpromising and underdelivering – which can result in shame and burnout, then shame for that. Getting out of a pattern of overworking takes faith that we will be OK outside of it. The fear of financial insecurity and what we would even do with unstructured time makes it a difficult bridge to cross – but if we can peel back slowly and let some space into our lives, we can explore how it would feel to have a bigger life in other areas. Perhaps areas outside of our control (the most difficult concept, because driving ourselves with overworking gives us a sense of control) and perhaps things we won't be able to execute perfectly on a first try – but what if we didn't have to be perfect? What if we didn't have to be extraordinary? Perhaps we still can be extraordinary – but we don't have to be, or to prove anything.

Urge-surfing

Learning to take a pause before acting on a feeling is one of the keystones of changing our behaviours. Urge-surfing is something we can do in the pause to strengthen our skills of observing an urge to do something we promised ourselves we wouldn't, rather than take it as a direct command.

Urges, like feelings, have a map, and if we gain the ability to experience them without acting upon them, we can find our way through them. We can see what might bring them on, how they build, where the different levels of intensity are and the patterns. Learning this landscape, we find out where the peak is, and experience the feeling of returning to the baseline after the urge has passed – which, like waves, all urges do. Ignoring it and pushing it down will make it come out the sides. Fighting sometimes can make it worse. It can feel like an endless thread that leads all the way to the same end, something growing and unstoppable. But we can become aware of it without attaching ourselves to it. We can accept its presence as simply a fact –

something bouncing off a feeling we don't want to feel right now that looks like a need to get out of our body. This is where we begin to ride it out, move with the wave until it subsides. It's a mindfulness exercise, where we develop a non-judgemental awareness of our thoughts, feelings, body and environment. It is taking things one single moment at a time, with an attitude of kindness towards ourselves. We don't have to shame ourselves for having it, we just have to experience it.

When you recognise an urge, put a timer on for twenty-five minutes. I was told, and eventually started to experience for myself, that an urge doesn't last longer than that if I don't spend that time obsessing over it, making a plot to fulfil it, moving myself closer to places where I am more likely to engage with it, or imagining how good I am going to feel once I do it.

It seemed almost insulting in its simplicity, like a well-meaning 'Have you tried not doing it?' from someone who doesn't know how it feels – but with practice it worked. We can step back and keep it simple – reducing our attention to the simple act of breathing. We can use distress-tolerance skills, box breaths, counting the lengths of our breaths and our grounding techniques. We can tell someone honestly, sharing its presence as a simple fact and not a doom prophecy. Escapism is human, so having a human connection helps.

Fighting the riptide exhausts you and pulls you further into it – but swimming parallel to the shore will take you out of the dangerous current, and you'll make it safely back.

Paired muscle relaxation that can help during urge surfing is a DBT skill that pairs your inhales and exhales with tensing and relaxing parts of your body.

Start from the head, going through the areas of the face one by one. Inhale, focus on a muscle group, tense it up, then relax it on the exhale. Knit and release your eyebrows, shut your eyes, squeeze your lips together and wrinkle your nose. Bring your shoulders to your ears and back down, clench and release your fists – on the exhale, visualise letting something go. Engage your core, legs, thighs and toes. Flex and point your feet. I finish with a full-body squeeze, and then do a couple of breaths where I hold my breath at the top of it.

Unless we are having a heart attack or a stroke, no matter the intensity, the feeling itself won't kill us. The more we practise not engaging in escapism behaviours, the more often the wolf we do not feed fucks off for a while. Urges come and go more quickly. The benefits grow and the space between the worst feeling imaginable and feeling on the right side of OK gets smaller. We can journal and document any changes to build up an evidence box of times it worked and the concrete proof.

If you are on a spiritual path, or growing along spiritual lines, these techniques can be used with prayer and meditation exercises, to reflect on acceptance, patience and connection. We can effectively channel our spiritual practice into making sane decisions, giving it the necessary practical aspect.

What's really going on here?

When we're not in crisis mode, we can have a look inside and ask questions, and answer them with integrity.

> What am I finding difficult to face right now?
> What am I scared to lose?
> What am I scared I will not get?

What am I trying to control?
What can I change?
What am I finding hard to accept?

We can ask ourselves 'What do I really need?' and work from there.

I want a moment to myself.
I want some peace.
I want to feel close to someone.
I want to feel safe.
I want to feel alive.

When we gain skill with managing intense urges, we can work on swapping out unloving behaviours for more constructive ones, and engaging with behaviours constructively rather than using them. Urges and impulses can be changed into actions, based on what we really want and need.

The hole in the soul is sometimes called 'the God-shaped hole'. In avoiding turning this into a theological argument, because it isn't one, God is simply a word I use to describe my beliefs – that I am not alone; there is something loving that is bigger than me, and I am a part of it. Some might call it a higher power. It can be the universe, or the ineffable connection I have with certain people. I don't know if it's true, but it helps me find greater meaning and act in my values when I act like it is. It isn't a thing that punishes or puppet-masters, it is simply an energy that reminds me I'm a human who belongs here, with the people I love, and that we should help each other. This principle of helping one another and being a part of something in the real world is the long-lasting treatment I've found for that rip in the fabric of my being.

Gratitude is a shift in perspective that turns what you have into enough

Recovery isn't supposed to be a dull and struggle-filled experience, and when it feels like it is, I can round it out by turning the magnifying glass onto things in my life that are actually OK.

Gratitude used to seem asinine to me, an exercise for other people who were blind to the reality of the world. However, my temperament swings easily to the misery line, and in my pursuit of not wanting to trundle along there, I was willing to try gratitude as an experiment.

Starting slow by writing down five things I was grateful for each day eventually grew, and I stopped having to look so hard for it. I realised it wasn't blinkers of positivity to deny my reality, it was warmth – looking for the areas in my life that comforted me in the middle of everything. I started saying thank you to the world when the traffic lights changed just as I approached them, an old friend reached out or something worked out when I didn't expect it to. Gratitude is best shared, so I shared it with other people, who then told me what they were grateful for, like their mum's health improvements and their cats feeling like freshly baked croissants as they cuddle up to them in the morning. Irritation stuck to me less, and I stopped letting things pass me by unappreciated. It allowed me to gravitate more towards things that gave me real-time joy. It may not have been a cure, but it was an antidote that I could have working alongside whatever else was going on. It was active – encouraging me to be a participant in the world around me, motivating me to act in line with the good in my life, to keep it around.

It grows, but it's still sometimes as small as saying, 'This is amazing,' in the shower when the water gets to the right temperature. Gratitude makes what I have feel like enough – something that feels so in opposition to addiction that it still takes my breath away.

PART III

Looking outwards – approaching your life from a more stable base.

VII. Getting into the World

But therapy can only get you so far. It's like the theory test when you're learning to drive. You can work out as much as you like on paper, but at some point you're going to have to get in the car and really fucking feel how it all works.
— Dolly Alderton,
Everything I Know About Love (2018)

When you want to be here, but also, what the fuck? When you aren't quite sure what your friendships are going to look like without drinking. When you thought you knew how to have fun, but your only hobby was setting fire to your life.

When I left home for university, my aunt wrote, 'Spread your wings, carefully,' in my card — pragmatic advice for a kid deviating off the farming path without much of a safety net. Rather than spreading my wings, I grew gills and became a strange creature at the bottom of the Mariana Trench, warped by a crushing darkness I grew steadily accustomed to.

When I got sober people told me being in recovery meant I could have a 'big life' – I could be an active participant in the world. This appealed to my inner megalomaniac, the part of me that thought more was better and most was best, that was born ambitious and hungry to taste the entire universe. It did not appeal to the part of me that wanted absolutely nothing to do with the world and felt like a loose thread in the tapestry of life.

Our relationship to the world is built in childhood. For the 'how-does-everyone-else-just-seem-to-get-it?' children, the 'life-became-catastrophically-unfair,-and-the-world-kept-turning-as-if-nothing-happened' children and the 'there-must-be-something-inherently-bad-about-me' children, the world can be a hostile place, which we must modify at a huge personal cost to fit into. Many of us became chameleons as a result of this, seeking approval, acceptance and safety under the guise of being someone else. We were talking about this in the trauma support group in New Haven that I joined just before I reached eighteen months sober. One of the members, an enviably aloof and mysterious art student from the Pacific Northwest, said that she just wished she knew how to act like a normal person. Another participant, a florist in her mid-forties who was more prone to saying 'pass' than participating, replied, tensely, that pretending to be 'normal' was killing her, and she just wished that she felt safe to be herself. I related to both women. I sometimes wished that I was normal, that I felt things a normal amount and that my reaction to the human condition wasn't violent acts of escapism. I used to wish I could drink 'like everyone else my age' – which is to say, without becoming angry, promiscuous, depressed or having ruined someone's wedding.

I also knew my fixation with being 'normal' was a futile mission that resulted in self-rejection. I was denying and shaming parts of myself that needed to be held close, given a cup of tea and told they aren't something that makes me fundamentally unlovable. But still, it felt too much to be 'too much' sometimes, like I would always be a square peg scrunched up into a round hole. It felt like the world was going to reject me whether I was drunk (because it was very clear, I did not drink in a way that was sane or safe) or sober (because, what the fuck? How can you not drink? How are you going to have a good time?).

As summer passed over into autumn in 2019 I passed the eighteen-months-sober mark, and though I still thought that a 26-year-old should have achieved more with their life, the idea that recovery was the hardest but most worthwhile thing I possibly could be doing was becoming less something I just said to make myself feel better, and more of a heartfelt belief. It was around this time that my Scottish friend, Gillian, called to tell me she was coming to New Haven to visit me. I was excited – my accent was fading and I needed some West Coast Scottish brutality, I'd started saying, 'Have a nice day!' to people (something my friends said made me 'basically American'). But it also carried dread. I had avoided telling her I'd been sober for eighteen whole months, and hid my recovery in the thousands of miles between us. We had drunk prolifically together, and I assumed that she would want to do so on this trip. I had to make a choice: abort my sobriety, lest my friend accuse me of giving up on my culture – or get honest. I sent a long and apologetic text saying I'd handed in my Scottish card with my choices, and I totally understood if she didn't want to come any more. The twisting agony in my guts stopped when she replied, 'Oh, thank God. You were a fucking nightmare when you drank.'

In her defence, I'd been kicked out of flats because I'd brought violent strangers home, and screamed down the intercom at 3 a.m. because I'd lost my keys. I had almost been declared a missing person in Italy when I ruined someone's twenty-first birthday by running off to do drugs with a bunch of Italian men. You know, just life-and-soul-of-the-party things.

When she told me she had been drinking less recently, because it was taking more than it gave and costing her more than money, I'd already mourned the friendship in an abandonment fantasy where she told me I wasn't fun any more. But she said she had better things to do than get drunk all the time: she was getting a PhD and had started seeing someone (who, four years later, she would marry, and I'd be the last person left on the dance floor).

When people hear I'm Scottish their first assumption is usually that I know how to drink. Which is correct – I was very good at it. I used to get a sense of pride and belonging from it. I'm not the only one; many North Americans often attribute their drinking to being of Irish, Scottish, Welsh or German descent. Australians, Russians and Central Europeans have statistical dominance in the league tables of the world's biggest drinkers. Some people say London is the alcoholics' paradise, and others say rural communities are where they really know how to drink. Every profession thinks they're the booziest industry. I thought as a musician I had everyone beat, but people in law, recruitment, the civil service, art, advertising, medicine and probably every other industry have thought the exact same thing, that in their industry, drinking is part of the job description.

'Like being Scottish, we drink,' I'd say. 'What else can we do with this weather?' I'd joke, and then drink. I'd drink, conforming to just one of the stereotypes that has punctuated people's opinions of us for political and financial gain, chipping away at the whole humanness of my nationality. Yes, the media made my accent synonymous with 'violent alcoholic' or a punchline that people imitate for their own entertainment, but it was a good excuse to drink – I wasn't doing anything that wasn't expected of me. It's the Celtic blood disorder, people told me, rather than acknowledging that deprived areas and the people in them are pushed to their emotional and psychological limits, and are given pubs and bookies rather than social change – a practice that has been going on for hundreds of years in different forms. It's easier for people to believe we're a nation of alcoholics who have it coming, rather than question why Scotland has the highest rate of suicide in the UK and no one wants to talk about it. I'd drink, and pretend I was having a really good time. 'We drink,' I'd say, 'it's what we do.' It's easier to mock drunk people doing drunk things on the news after football matches, or be really fucking proud of the fact that I am a woman who can drink like a man because that's how Scottish people drink, than really question why we drink to die. The fact that I continued to drink felt wrong to me. Irvine Welsh said in an interview, 'We've been fucked up for so long that sobriety is actually the new getting fucked up.' Me and my friend, being two Scottish women having the desire to investigate our drinking habits, rather than subscribing unquestioningly to something we were just supposed to do, felt strangely rebellious. Not against our culture or country, which is so important to me outside of anything to do with alcohol, but against the idea imposed upon us that we had to settle for destructive drinking as something that brings us together, when it didn't feel like it used to. I'd accepted a convenient stereotype that was used against me and my country, and I was done with that story. So many of us are.

It also got me thinking of other areas of my life I could question and investigate. I could explore what I actually enjoyed doing, what mattered to me, how I could show up for the people I loved and what I wanted out of my brief time here.

I've had a lot of experience pretending to be other people, so it's about time I practise being myself

As I continued to do the inside work of assessing my struggles, blind spots, assets and desires, I realised it wasn't all work I could do in my head. I needed to get out into the world. I could float in my room, like an orca in SeaWorld, or I could find my corner of the ocean, to ride with the pull of the waves, sink yachts and sing with my pod. I didn't want to keep creating my personal SeaWorld. I didn't want to believe the world was a hostile, scary place where I didn't belong any more – or at least not all of it. There's only so much you can do theoretically, by imagining what it might look like. The self-knowledge and insight we gain from recovery are made more potent when we take them outside of our heads and make some new experiences.

It's hard to motivate yourself for something you don't know the outcome of, but I could repurpose my resilience as a woman that just wouldn't die into my desire to live more authentically. I could live in line with the self that I didn't have to contort myself to be, and shape my life, the people in it and the things I spent time doing from that place.

Initially, drinking was a way of feeling like I was accessing the most truthful version of myself and the life I wanted, until it destroyed everything I loved. I needed to work out how to do it sober. Pretending to be someone else will only align you with a life that you do not want to live, and when you're sober you can't ignore that.

When you stop abandoning yourself and really connect to yourself truthfully, you start to discover the substance of who you are. Undeniable aspects of yourself become known to you, and you begin to uncover the authentic self that has been there all along, though it was sometimes hidden and sometimes suppressed.

Authenticity changes from a feeling to an experience with action. 'Move a muscle, change a thought' isn't only a practice for tidying your room when living in squalor is chipping away at your desire to exist. The confidence-building exercise of doing the authentic thing reinforces who you are, what you stand for and the world you want to be a part of. When you live and act in line with your authentic self you get to make even more new discoveries about the truth of yourself, outside of the worn patterns of shame. Your old limiting thoughts and beliefs about yourself change and your confidence grows, from wearing the outfit you really want to wear, to leaving an unhappy relationship that fits in with the socially acceptable relationship model; from choosing to stand by what is right even when it makes you unpopular, to deciding to trust someone, staying sober or sticking to a boundary you made with yourself when it would be easier to break it. Being your authentic self means that you are something that no one can take away from you, and it's so much easier to remember what you said when you aren't lying all the time.

It doesn't mean there will not be consequences or a backlash – but the growth of authenticity and trusting yourself and your values means you develop the personal power to be unmoved by them.

Acting upon authenticity reminds you that you are not just a mishmash of negative attributes and trauma responses – you are an entire human being, with traits, temperament, some things you've picked up along the way, quirks, likes, dislikes and assets. You are always in the process of being yourself with no landing point – it's eternally ongoing, and authenticity opens so many avenues for discovery. I thought all along I needed to be normal, and to get rid of the thing that was wrong with me, and authenticity tells me that while there is work to do, I'm just another human, on planet Earth, doing her best.

Looking at ourselves non-judgementally, we can see things about ourselves that we may have missed when we were wanting to be better, further along or entirely different. We can act in accordance with our attributes to strengthen them. We can start small, until we are ready to accept and integrate the parts we are a bit more uncomfortable with, like being more introverted than most people, the fact that we might see the world a bit differently or a stance that might be misunderstood. What matters is that we are giving ourselves the feedback that who we are is acceptable, and belongs somewhere.

The challenge of embodying the values we wish to express in the world doesn't always have an immediate payoff, but the commitment has depth and can become something to depend on. We worry less about the things we're not when we're invested in and appreciating the things that we are. What's more, think of all the people we love for their authenticity, and how the bravery of being ourselves can help other people be themselves.

I realised I didn't want to be normal, I wanted to be me. If I became weirder in the process of becoming whole, so be it.

But why would I bother being authentic in a world that is authentically bullshit?

Getting sober means existing in a world I didn't plan to be alive for. Earlier generations lived through their own horrors – wars, lobotomies, epidemics, famines, genocide. Our generation didn't invent trauma or despair, but we have more access, more news, more overwhelm, more hopelessness, modern challenges – not helped by the fact that we have to enter survival mode simply to exist, as the demands on us and the cost of living increase and wages do not.

The more I observe the dysfunction of the world, the more I appreciate that I can't and don't want to assimilate to become 'normal', because aside from it not existing, none of this is very normal, and none of us is particularly OK. I often don't feel equipped to handle this world, or to fix it. The reality is, I am not equipped to fix it. I can't reverse climate change by myself. I don't understand AI or comprehend what it will do to the world, I can't stop wars and money is still an absolute mystery to me. I must accept that I, as an individual, do not have the skills to save the entire planet. But I cannot fall into hopelessness, because I do have skills, a big heart, and a hunger for change and justice. I have the willingness to be a part of something and join in, in the ways I can. I alone can't save the world, but I can make tiny changes to it. I can engage in my community and help people who need me. I can do what must be done to say what must be said, and assess each situation to see where my skills can be put to use, for the action-based hope of one day leaving the Earth better than I found it.

Sobriety means I'm neither ignoring it, nor considering it a lost cause for which my contribution is pointless. I don't love my friends because they change the entire world, I love them because they do what they can in their sphere of influence – in our world of shared space. It doesn't have to be enormous, it doesn't have to be marketable or broadcastable. It's meeting a friend to support them when their dad is sick, listening to someone who is struggling, doing someone a favour like picking up their post, signing a petition, volunteering time when I have no money and donating money when I have no time, joining a protest, using my skills where they're needed, supporting a friend's new endeavour, educating myself carefully, having uncomfortable conversations, listening, organising, using my voice and realising I will always be part of something much bigger than I know, and it is so much better to get involved. We all change the world in our own way, with our own set of vital skills. When you abandon 'normal' and are working outside of expectations and blueprints, you can be a childless, freelance, unmarried renter – and still be exactly where you need to be, doing necessary work to try to leave the world better than we found it.

To be open, aware and curious, it helps to be present

So many of us don't even recognise our anxiety any more because it has become our baseline – and the world responds with 'Have you tried yoga?' Then we have to hurry our healing, because this world moves so fast, and can feel so demanding. Alcohol is marketed as a blanket for an overloaded central nervous system, to slow us down and temper our overstimulation.

We can't afford to simply be one person, with our jobs, social media presence and side hustles. We are syphoned off into a constant state of multitasking, with notifications incessantly demanding immediacy out of us. It is renegade behaviour to wait more than twenty-four hours to reply to an email and a huge statement to ignore our phone even on holiday. Our presence is bled over all of our devices and the constant availability we're expected to have for everyone in our lives. The zombie mode of either drinking around the world or trying to keep up with it in a manic state of dissociation is very convenient for a society that doesn't benefit from questioning the way things are or simply being present for it. Modern life, capitalism and consumer culture depend on us not being present, because we are told that the comfort we are looking for is in the potential purchases, prestige and property we get targeted ads for from the moment we open our eyes.

No one can monetise presence, because it's something already in us, and it doesn't require a synthetic manipulation of our endogenous opioid system for profit. There is no urgency of 'You need this *now*' in presence, and doing the very next thing that needs to be done slowly and intentionally doesn't have a financial incentive.

The idea of being present felt like a punishment to me at first. I worried that if I stopped for a single second, I would be faced with the cataclysm of every single thing in my head, something that had always made me very thirsty. In his modern classic *The Power of Now* (1997), Eckhart Tolle offers a technique to stop racing thoughts: 'Try a little experiment. Close your eyes and say to yourself slowly and deliberately: "I wonder what my next thought is going to be." Then become very alert and wait for the next thought.'

It was fun to practise, because sometimes it worked. It created a small window that reminded me that, as Michael Alan Singer in *The Untethered Soul* (2007) says, 'You are not the voice in your head, you're the one who hears it.' I was consciously aware of the next thought, and could turn my attention to it, rather than let it take me over, which is useful for someone who has seven years of thoughts in two minutes. The more I experimented with it, and felt quiet seconds of peace in the listening, it created a genuine desire for presence, to be wholly and undeniably in the exact moment I was in, rather than all the stories, narratives, worries and ruminations.

When I felt myself in a thousand places at once, I experimented with turning my attention to exactly where my feet and hands were, intimately making contact with where I was and what I was doing. When I travelled to Seattle for my first sober solo trip in 2019, I challenged myself to be there, and only there. With the curiosity I was developing and the bravery I felt, I did and saw everything I'd wanted to do and see since I was a grungy teenager. I found and met up with other sober people to spend time in my favourite place on Earth: twenty-four-hour diners. I was there for every burnt coffee and midnight pancakes, witnessing the quiet moments in people's complex lives.

When I returned to New Haven I carried this practice with me. Usually I darted in and out of my favourite coffee shop each morning as if I was on my way to save lives, but my first morning back I listened to an enthusiastic conversation between the barista and a customer in front of me, about how coincidental it was that they had both performed at the Royal Albert Hall, she as a teenage chorister and he as a DJ. Their conversation was animated and friendly, and finished with a 'See you next week!' as he walked over to his table. Their conversation meant I waited longer than I normally would have – something my need for immediacy can turn into fury – but it wasn't an inconvenience. I didn't actually have anywhere to be in any hurry, I was just used to charging from place to place to maximise the amount of time I could spend working or scrolling. I had always had a soft spot for 'chatty people', probably from having a childhood where trips to the supermarket took two and a half hours longer than expected because my mum would bump into people she knew, which in a small town was everyone. I have an uncle who walks down the street of his village, simply to find someone to ask about their day. Anywhere my dad goes he usually does a lap of the room to see who he knows. At my graduation from Yale in the USA he found himself sitting next to someone from Dumfries, the town over from us in Scotland. He seeks community and somehow it always seeks him back. Maybe I could be a chatty person too, maybe I already had it in me, I just needed to uncover it more. Waiting for the conversation in front of me to finish in the coffee shop, I actually read the flyers pinned on the community notice board by the menu for a community choir with donation-based membership, free cycling lessons for adults, a breakdown of the importance of local housing authorities and steps we can take to protect them, a free art show and pay-what-you-can yoga. I hadn't even read or even really noticed there was a community noticeboard before, but had said to so many people it was hard to make friends as an adult.

Practising presence and authenticity challenged the idea that I'd always struggled to make friends. While it was true that in the past it had been difficult, as an adult I had to believe the simple fact that there were many out there like me, and I could seek them. I took up a pole-dancing class (I came to find out this is an unavoidable rite of passage for sober women looking for a sober hobby), and a girl asked if she could have my number – she was looking for friends in town. It became less preposterous to introduce myself to people at gigs and gym classes, which made me go to more gigs and gym classes, go to a shop rather than buying something online, and actually show up to gatherings where I gradually got to know the people who also frequented them. Finding out who you are around other people is often a lot more interesting than finding out who you are by yourself, because working things out relationally is so deeply human and so vital for our humanity.

One of my harshest realities was that alcohol did not make me a good friend

Keeping friends after getting sober gives you the opportunity, in real time, to find out who you are without a drink in your hand. There were friends who accepted me, and were quick to believe and understand to the best of their ability why I couldn't have alcohol in my life any more. Acting authentically draws these people closer, those who make you feel seen, supported and energised after spending time together, who take you as you are but don't take your shit, and who have the bravery to be honest. They do not have jealousy or superiority as their first response, belittle choices you make for yourself, selectively approve of you based on the company you keep, enable you because it's easier than a healthy confrontation, or remind you of your shame or pain to keep you small. You may have the same conflicts and confusions that all adult friendships have, but most importantly, these are the people you don't need to drink to be around.

It's OK to admit that drinking with people was fun. A lot of my pub pals are still my pals – the only difference is, we don't drink together any more and are all growing in our own way. With some of them I found a deeper connection, where we were both freer to be who we were as a person and friend, which is a lot easier when you're not ending the night needing an exorcism on the bathroom floor. I found out more about my friends in sobriety than I did through our entire friendship – you have time for that when you're not doing hangover admin for 50 per cent of your life. Most of them still drink, and I had to realise that the reasons I drank weren't like theirs, and that my drinking wasn't anything to do with theirs. Their relationship with alcohol was their own journey, and not a commentary on mine as much as their drinking wasn't a commentary on my sobriety.

When my unhealthy relationship with alcohol was illuminated, it exposed some of my unhealthy relationship with some of my friends. There were some I kept around simply because it kept me in certain environments, and some that I was scared of, never quite sure where I stood with them. Detrimental friendships drifting apart is a natural consequence of growing up, and sobriety sometimes speeds up the process. Some resented me for not drinking, because they took it as a reflection on them, or they didn't believe it was possible for me to do that. Some just liked having me around as an example of 'Well, I'm not as bad as Lauren.' There was judgement and stakes placed on my sobriety, which came solely from their own discomfort. I can't process that for them, but I can be a soft landing if they ever want to talk about it. In sobriety you get to decide how you want to be treated, and as long as your expectations are reasonable, it works out better for everyone involved. I still love the friends I lost – it wasn't wasted time or love; we were there for each other for a period of our lives, and those friends aren't now disposable just because our paths diverged.

Friendship loss is hard, but I was already living without my first best friend – the one I thought I could never live without – bottom-shelf vodka and all its dependable companions. It always there for me when all others let me down. It was my protector, and I loved it for everything it did for me when I didn't know what else to do. For my own safety, like any relationship that isn't working, I had to leave, grieve what I lost and what never was.

Boredom is a trigger for escapism

In the early days I wanted to drink to make mundane tasks more 'interesting', like wanting a swig of vodka to make brushing my teeth more thrilling – it was hard to accept that some things were just boring. But still, I once said to a friend that I was bored and she replied, 'Well, your life is very boring.' She was right: all I did was work and worry.

My friendship with Vic, a yoga teacher from Essex, started over a shared love of chain-smoking and complaining. We're an oddly matched pair; there is a 100 per cent chance that if you see us, I'll be wearing one of my seven black lounge suits, and Vic will be wearing vintage leopard-print flares, a pink fur jacket and a 'Will travel for disco' hat. The night we flew late to Berlin for a long weekend, she went to Berghain and I went to bed, with Käsespätzle. We wouldn't have met under any circumstances other than recovery, considering Vic loved nightlife and I loved drinking room-temperature vodka by myself.

The main thing we had in common was that we were two sober women in our twenties trying to work out what we enjoyed, after realising that not caring whether you lived or died wasn't as glamorous as we thought, and drinking your way around continental Europe isn't a personality trait.

'Honestly, I couldn't tell the difference between fun and chaos,' Vic says. 'The only way I knew how to have fun was setting my central nervous system on fire. Getting sober, I felt like fun had been stolen from me, and [I'd] started taking myself too seriously and [sobriety] made my life small. I had romantic ideas of my drinking and just thought the cost of being sober was that I'd just never enjoy myself again. I didn't think I could do anything any more. If you were watching sports, you were supposed to be drinking; if you were doing something arty, it was drugs; if you were going out, it was both.'

We're used to asking other people what they do for fun, or scrambling for some answers when we are asked, but it's very rare we ask ourselves what we do for fun.

'I didn't want to be miserable any more, so I started slowly experimenting with what I found fun. I realised I missed music, dancing and going out. I didn't know if I could still do that as a sober person, whether I'd have the confidence.'

When we practise authenticity, we can check our motives for things, and ask ourselves why we are doing things, truly.

'I realised the real reason I liked going out – it was the music, getting dressed up, living outside of the day-to-day, being playful and creative with my make-up, deciding where to go, getting excited about who I would see – none of that was drugs or alcohol. Still, it took me a long time to go back into the spaces of going out, and I had to find the right people and take care of my recovery first. I didn't immediately know how to go to clubs and festivals and not take a ton of drugs, so being around people who could do that without ruining their life sucked the joy out of it. But I found people who wanted what I wanted, and started to enjoy myself again.'

Some of us get sober and realise we're more 'staying in' sober than 'going out' sober, and for some people it's the other way around. But that doesn't limit or prohibit us from being in any particular category of person.

'Something I love is asking myself what type of fun I need,' says Vic. 'Do I need to be around friends who understand me deeply, sitting on the couch and watching YouTube, or do I want to dance, stay up late and see new DJs? It's all fun to me – the fun I need on a Saturday night is different from the fun I need after a stressful day at work. The fun isn't an enormous chemical change; it's being in a space that makes me feel alive, it's feeling connected, it's music. It's not exactly escapism – it's forgetting yourself for a few hours, not being a person with a job and responsibilities. It's feeling young.'

A lot of us can feel like our youth was stolen from us by trauma, growing up too fast, drugs, alcohol and maladaptive coping mechanisms. Having fun is a type of play that is necessary for people in recovery.

'As a survivor of so many things, it's a triumph to feel pleasure. As a person in recovery, it's a triumph to know you can forget yourself and all your worries, but not self-abandon. I can go and be in a space and not care what people think about me. That's a triumph for someone who takes themselves too seriously. I did myself a huge amount of damage – it's necessary to repair it with play and enjoyment. The beginning is a learning curve.'

Early on in our friendship Vic told me about one of her friends who said that in the form he filled out before he moved into a sober-living facility they asked him to write down what he enjoyed. The only two things he could think of were: 'The colour blue and Ibiza.' We cackled at this, but when we asked ourselves what we would have said, Vic's would have been 'taking ecstasy and having sex with strangers' and mine was 'cutting myself and hoping the next swipe on the dating app falls in love with me'.

'You have to try shit, try stuff you don't enjoy – how else would I know I don't enjoy badminton? Enjoy the feeling of having choices. We put ourselves in boxes with fear of failure, so give yourself the permission to try things and have it not work out. You can take recovery seriously without taking yourself too seriously. Letting go of who you thought you were lets you see who is underneath.'

A lot of the time the process of working out who you are involves sitting with the pain, processing arcane wounds and doing the hard thing, the thing you don't want to do. Working out who you are is facing your shadow-side, and accepting the thing you thought was unacceptable about yourself. It is having things taken from you before you are ready and learning to live with it. It's often said that pain is the touchstone of progress. With a bit of time and experience, joy can become a touchstone of progress. Play is a touchstone of progress and growth for people who never got to have fun as a kid.

On our last day in Berlin we went around a gallery, and took pictures of ourselves trying to recreate the poses in paintings. We laughed at how much alcoholic admin we'd have to do if we'd been drinking on this trip, replacing lost passports, trying to negotiate our way out of trouble and doing damage control in a foreign language, and managing Berlin-level comedowns. We were set to go out on our last night but were both a bit tired. Someone mentioned there was a really good spa on the outside of town – a quick Uber ride later, and we were sitting in a sauna, rubbing our bodies with salt as a woman leading a citrus ritual beat walls of heat around the space with a towel.

Later that year I made friends with some neighbours and we organised a trip to Leipzig together. On the balcony of the Airbnb I remembered being in Amsterdam, on a similar balcony, drunk and high. I asked myself if I was having as much fun this time around, sober. I waited honestly for an answer as we made a stew with pomegranate and lamb. I bathed naked in a lake by a sauna near the edge of town, then dried myself in the sun, laughter coming to me without effort as I was rocked by a swinging chair. I went to museums, read books by rivers and sat with my friends at a kitchen table playing card games and wondering what shoegaze was. I stood on the balcony and my heart said, 'Yes, and there's no comedown.'

When I told Vic about it she said, 'It's funny, one day you're crying because you think your life is over because you're sober, and then the most fun you've ever had in your life is because of it.'

What is fun for you?

Do what you can to have fun. If you have no money, make time. If you have money, spend some of it to make the time you're not working fun. If you have no time or money, use the last half-hour of the day enjoying the busy life you're fighting for, even if it's just one intentional act of enjoyment. Every human needs half an hour to relax every day. If you're busy, it's a whole hour.

It's amazing how much time you free up when you're not wasting your life in futile attempts to fill a bucket with a hole in it – and how that time can be used. At first, I was simply trying to keep my hands busy to not harm myself, but then I was processing my experiences through creative, physical or intellectual activities, or curiously trying things I didn't think I had the time or patience for. I could feel the sustainable thrill of being interested in something, and the pleasure in that. I rediscovered reading, and eventually writing – doing things I truly loved and lost along the way. It gave me things to talk about with people, and being a founding member of a book club. This extended to all sorts of interests, such as painting (it's good to have a hobby you're bad at; you can't monetise it), rollerblading (I was the most sober person there and I fell the most) and joining a poetry club. Get a pet, get into fitness, take cold showers, go wild swimming, play The Sims, learn to knit, go to grad school, train to be a therapist, write Notes-app poetry, do contact sports, live out your childhood dreams, catch bugs in the forest. None of it is off-limits when you're sober.

Spurts of enthusiasm don't have to be pathologised away. You can really enjoy painting one day and be obsessed with crocheting the next. It doesn't have to be a bad thing that you get really into rock climbing and six months later cancel your membership, or your walking-in-the-forest-every-day era is now a monthly thing – what matters is that in every stroke, stitch, hold or foot crunching on a leaf, you are there, and thrilled about it; that it gives you a sense of aliveness, which gives you enough life energy to answer all your fucking emails. You'll find that some things stick.

With the friends you keep, make a conscious effort to still spend time with them outside of situations where drinking is the main event. You can be creative with how you spend time together. In the early stages it might help to have a transparent conversation with some friends. Some can be supportive, some of them might not see the inner catastrophic emotional consequences, and can innocently ask if we're being a wee bit dramatic. None of them know what you need from them, unless you tell them. You can be clear whether you feel fine and just want to enjoy your Diet Coke in peace, or whether you need some sensitivity around some topics or places. As close as you are, they can't predict what you're feeling or where you're at, and I can confirm that there's no stage of sobriety where people gain the ability to read your mind and immediately know what to do. All you can control is being as honest as you can and accepting their answer, whatever stage of understanding they are at.

If you're going to a social event that is centred around drinking, ask yourself what your motive is to be there. Ask yourself what you want out of it, what you can bring to it, if you have the energy for it and whether it is an opportunity to connect or disconnect. We don't have to operate from a position of 'no', but we are allowed to say no to things. If we have survived abuse dynamics, we can have an inbuilt response to just tolerate discomfort in order to mitigate future retaliation – it can induce a sense of danger around our 'no'. But in trusted company we can have faith that it will be received and accepted. It can help us develop a sense of agency and the ability to be assertive in our choices.

Being present is tiring, so work out ways you can show up and not go past your social limit. Plan your own transport, and have a trusted friend to call, someone to go with who you can be authentic with. Get comfortable with taking breaks, even if it's to cheekily vape in the bathroom.

Whenever I go to an event I normally have a minimum amount of time I am willing to stay, and anything beyond that is a bonus. Usually, with this flexible attitude, I am more likely to stay longer than my time boundary, as I often find myself having a better time than I anticipated. If that isn't the case, or I have met my threshold, I have a simple rule of leaving as soon as I stop having fun. It doesn't have to be all or nothing – you can go for half the night, stay for the act you want to see, have a seat and find a quiet space.

If you're in a mandatory fun situation (work event, non-negotiable party, etc.), embrace the joy of leaving. The ultimate reward is when you get to leave somewhere, and simply be really weird by yourself in the comfort of your own home. After an endurance task of a day or an event, I usually plan a bath, my favourite show, something delicious to eat or something absolutely mind-numbing before bed – as a treat for being a human when I didn't want to be.

In our workplaces we might not get to be ourselves; we are usually disconnected by obligations, tensions and teams – so drinking is often the only way of 'getting together' that isn't a horrendous team-building exercise. Drinking also surrounds the only things that make work bearable, like gossip, complaining about your job and having sex with your coworkers. I can assure you, from experience, you can do all of those things sober.

We are adults in the workplace. If we are grown up enough to handle money, responsibilities and people, then we are adult enough to advocate for our needs at work. Workplace boundaries can feel like a hard thing to draw, as we can sometimes feel indebted, especially if we have a thread of imposter syndrome running through us. We need to understand our value in the workplace, and our value as a worker who works better sober. Furthermore, we can have the added joy of knowing exactly what we said to every single person at Christmas parties and after-work drinks.

Around milestones and calendar events that intersect with drinking, make your own meaning, your own ritual. Use your authenticity: if you are creative, use your skills to imagine something unique; if you are organised, you can utilise that to make something special with other people involved; if you are a chaos demon, do something so unusual that you won't forget it.

One of the most underrated things about recovery is actually experiencing things for the first time. People in recovery are always marvelling over simple things: our first sober relationship, sexual encounter, conflict resolution and every variety of social event. We have a sense of pride over it, and a new delight in the taste of an orange, baths, drinking enough water and keeping a houseplant alive. It seems childlike, but being as present and innocent as a child discovering the world around me is something I treasure. It's the opportunity to feel everything for the first time the second time around, this time appreciating how much it actually all means.

Let the world change you for the better. It mashed me up before, and now I'm going to build mine back up with love. I'm going to challenge my ideas, do things that scare me and risk being uncomfortable, because I have no idea what's going to happen, and it might not be terrible.

VIII. The Internet

Most people know how it feels to be online with an aching heart.

– Amy Liptrot, *The Instant* (2022)

When you grew up terminally online, hyper-self-aware and not quite sure where you belong. When you feel like you need to fit a certain role, dress size and image to belong. When you spend all day talking to people, but feel so fucking alone.

Before my friends from music school in Glasgow came to visit the countryside I grew up in, I showed them some videos from a rural childhood – like sheepdog trials (a dog guides four sheep through a series of obstacles and is marked on speed and accuracy) and agricultural shows, where sheep, cows and baking get judged while we mill about a field eating burgers from vans. After about twenty minutes of this, one said, 'I can see why you really loved the internet.'

My parents very radically had no expectation that I would

continue the farming tradition, perhaps to save themselves the struggle of trying to convince me. I admired farmers – how they greeted each other at markets with familiar handshakes, speaking their own language of agriculture, remembering the minute details of each other's lives. I wanted my parents' work ethic, with their commitment to taking care of the countryside, their heartfelt dedication and their ability to tell tomorrow's weather from the way the sheep were standing next to the dry-stone dykes that were made by my ancestors over a hundred years ago. But I was a kid who grew up wanting to be an actress, poet and It-girl. I grew up writing short stories about a future where I moved to New York and only ate apples because I couldn't afford anything else (having actually done this now, it wasn't as much fun as I'd imagined), but that was a small sacrifice for the benefit of living in a city, where I'd never have to spend another spring in the lambing shed.

Growing up, I wasn't a townie or a young farmer. I was equally uncomfortable at events where people raced to shear a sheep, drink a pint and eat a pie as I was at sleepovers with girls my own age. The former were too loud, and I'd just discovered Anne Sexton, so I was precocious and insufferable. At the latter I'd feel like the third friend, the one they could live without. I'd make up interesting secrets about myself to gain favour with girls who, knowing I have a shark phobia, would force me to watch *Jaws* and stuffed my pyjama bottoms with tampons as I slept, after discovering that I hadn't started my period yet.

Then somewhere in my childhood the family computer got the internet. Initially it scared me. I'd run to warn my parents that I'd opened a malevolent portal if I ever accidentally double-clicked on the icon. But then I started 'going on the computer', denying the household the use of the phone. The dial-up sounds became my *New World Symphony*. I fought my childhood anxieties by trying to be a big deal on Neopets. We didn't have family abroad or go on big holidays, so looking at pictures of Japan and Australia felt like real-life science-fiction, and I fed my creativity with websites like All Poetry and message boards for my favourite bands, where I wrote and shared things with people who felt things as largely as I did.

The internet was my refuge. It was pain management, the perfect escape – just keep searching for the next interesting thing. There was no place more wonderful, when you didn't want to be where you were but couldn't be anywhere else. In many ways it was my first drug. I accidentally deleted it from the desktop once and panicked that I had lost my lifeline to the world where I made sense – the same level of devastation as realising the bag is empty, but you don't feel finished.

The early internet was an unmonitored wasteland, but it was my wasteland, and there weren't any ads. We had no idea what the word algorithm meant, and personal branding wasn't even a concept – we were just freaks expressing ourselves. I could find places to articulate myself in words and be as weird as I wanted, and people actually praised me rather than bullied me for it. Being ostracised at school didn't sting as much when I had this corner that felt like mine. It carried me before I knew drinking was an option. There was a magical time for every internet user, before you accidentally opened a link to a cartel beheading someone or you got groomed for the first time.

My initial fears started to seem like a premonition, as young people were taken advantage of, identities were stolen and hate speech, cyberbullying and malicious networks were given a place to intensify. Exploitation and crime had new worlds that required separate divisions to deal with them, because we had no idea how far and fast this would go. It belonged in the hands of the next generation; we taught our parents how it worked – there was no one to guide us. People who knew that would take advantage of us, and, God, we were so vulnerable.

Our brains were in the early stages of their development, and what felt like limitless possibility was now limitless envy, fear, information we had no business knowing and consciousness of how we were perceived. We had to rank our top eight friends, for fuck's sake. We had the entire world opened to us and, in our most insecure years, so much more to compare ourselves to.

We don't always talk about eating disorders in recovery, so I'm going to

The idea that thinness meant acceptance was well established before social media. There were already entire magazines promoting unregulated, low-calorie diet plans next to women's bodies they were holding up either to ridicule or present as the 'ideal' figure we could achieve if we were good enough. Online, young people with a deep desire to feel better, different and more worthy created the pro-ana (shortened from pro-anorexia) chatrooms and forums that, at age 13, I was avidly engaged with. We shared how we kept our practices secret in the family home and managed the faintness, dizziness and rage that extreme hunger created, while sharing 'thinspiration' and pictures of our ribs to affirm, 'This is worth it.' We didn't fit in, but we could fit into smaller dress sizes. If I couldn't be seen for who I was, I wanted to be invisible or perfect. I took my body into my own hands, and kept it as tiny as I possibly could.

We were teenagers trying to make sense of the world, repeating, 'Nothing tastes as good as skinny feels' (a quote popularised by Kate Moss — something she has expressed regret over) in the hope that we had found something that might make us feel good about ourselves. Sometimes it was about thinness — we all wanted to look like Effy in *Skins* — and sometimes it was about the addictive feeling of something we could control, and have something we were proud of, even if it was a potentially fatal mental illness. It gave us a sense of meaning. If the rest of the world didn't understand, it was because they didn't know how good it felt to 'not care whether you died, as long as you were buried in a size-zero coffin', and how good it felt to type that into a message board and have people reply with, 'Hungry to bed, hungry to rise, makes a girl skinny in size.'

I didn't hate food, I feared it. I was obsessed with it. Feeling unworthy of it, I rejected it, not even wanting to touch dairy products in case their high calorie content got into my system through my fingertips. When I was 14 I realised there were other ways to reject food and still experience it, and so I fell into the anorexia-bulimia pipeline.

Already a young classical musician — something that exists at the intersection of perfection and obsession — I was easy prey for an eating disorder, but there are many other risk factors. Impulsivity, emotional dysregulation, escapism and a history of mental-health issues all heighten the risk. These are, unsurprisingly, also risk factors for substance abuse. Eating-disorder charity Beat reports that 50 per cent of people with eating disorders use alcohol or drugs, a rate five times higher than the general population. Approximately 35 per cent of individuals who were dependent on alcohol or other drugs also have eating disorders, a rate eleven times greater than the general population.[1]

However, eating disorders and addiction are secretive, insidious and work in the shadows where statistics can't find them. So many people don't know they have disordered eating, as early-2000s media and current 'wellness' trends package it as an esteemable choice, even when it is controlling us.

Between the age of 25 and 26, the first two years of my recovery, my most secret shame was the return of my bulimia. When I started using substances they accelerated past my disordered eating and displaced it; they gave me something else to believe in. When you're sober you're reminded of exactly how it feels to sit in a body you despise. More aware than ever of the emptiness, I went on binges for when I needed to feel full. The ritual of experiencing comfort, then rejecting it on my terms by purging, soothed any disappointment or fear over what I couldn't control. Having a bit more money and privacy as an adult, it was easier. I could work my schedule around it, because it was my entire schedule. Eventually I wasn't just purging after binges. I had my favourite public toilets all over town, so I was never caught with any meal in my stomach that I needed out of me. I had it down to an art – I could purge without making a sound, like an Olympic diver entering the water without a splash.

I saw images online of sober people talking about the health benefits of sobriety, how it enhanced their yoga and sleep, and reduced their risk of cancer, and I was somehow falling down a deeper hole. I couldn't seem to find an inspirational quote to stick on a pastel background as I was trying to convince myself not to stick my fingers down my throat or lie about already having had dinner, and trying to find a filter that hid my puffy face and red knuckles.

Media depictions of bulimia happen off-camera, alluding to it with a thin woman looking sadly into a toilet bowl. It's rarely portrayed as the violent act against the body that it is. It's rarely acknowledged that the very feeling of it is addictive, and the feeling of not doing it gives you the fear of God. Bulimia isn't always taken as seriously as anorexia. It can be seen as its little cousin, despite the mortality rate being almost exactly the same (4.0 per cent for anorexia and 3.9 per cent bulimia).[2] As a bulimic, I just felt like a failed anorexic, and I didn't know it was a problem because weight loss is usually met with approval. No one cares about your eating disorder if you're above a certain weight threshold – I could convince myself I was just trying to do what the magazine said would make me happy.

I tried not to purge on the days that I performed – it's not easy to sing after rinsing your throat with acid – but when I could no longer keep that promise to myself I was reminded of my rock bottom with alcohol and drugs, and joined a support group for people with eating disorders. Immediately upon entering the windowless, terracotta-coloured room in the New Haven Health Centre, which was devoid of any character and always a tiny bit too warm, I sized up everyone's body, as they did mine – some more subtly than others. Eating disorders are many things, but if they are one thing, it is competitive. But there was a shared understanding that we were there, even if we didn't want to be, because we wanted to get better. We weren't doing the work to win the fight, we were stepping out of the fight and finding something different. Like with sobriety – it was changing tracks.

Gripping to the handrails of something hopeful, I accepted

that my journey was going to look a little bit different from the more typically inspirational pastel ones I saw online. Maybe they were going through the same thing, too, but were really good at using Canva. Like drugs and alcohol, regardless of what my eating disorder had taken from me, I was still alive, and I still had a chance to take the suggestions and follow someone's expertise and experience. I shared honestly, even the unspeakable things, like being scared that if I recovered from my eating disorder I would miss it, because it was the only thing that gave me a sense of accomplishment. All the work I had done so far in my recovery started to alchemise in this area, because I had come out of denial. Having spent two years working on myself, I knew how to experience discomfort, and knew, undeniably, that if you use your tools over time, things begin to change. Slowly, things improved, just like they had done with alcohol and drugs. It's harder, though not impossible, to purge with long nails, so I grew them out long and almond shaped, as a symbol of my decision to change. I let my weight rise and fall without writing it down in a notebook. I ate butter again, and it tasted good.

Online I was used to scrutinising every picture of myself as if I were on trial for the crime of having a human body. There were only about five pictures in existence of my body below my shoulders because I couldn't bear it being photographed – any time I saw the words '[Some well-meaning person] has tagged you in a picture', I wanted to call the police. I was encouraged to look at my body and state facts about it non-judgementally. I practised this in my bedroom mirror for many days, looking for curiosity rather than condemnation. I thought my thighs were quite disproportionate ('By what standards?' I ask myself now), but they were strong. My shoulders were broad, and eventually

I started to like that about myself. I didn't have to feel beautiful (why do I have to be beautiful anyway, and by what standards?), I just had to walk in acceptance with the body I had. Weirdly, it made me feel very beautiful. I asked Nicholas if there was such a thing as reverse body dysmorphia, because I was starting to look in the mirror and not hate myself. He suggested it might just be self-esteem. Dropping my judgements of myself helped me drop my judgements of other people, and I stopped viewing the world based on the worthiness of my body compared to other people's. I was leaving that struggle behind and walking in the real world, where there was so much more on offer than the places I wanted to hide in.

We have so much accessible information now about what eating disorders are and their dangers. People share their stories of recovery and the possibility of living outside the things we learned coming of age in the early 2000s. We can more easily spot a trend that is designed to make us obsess over the 52 calories that make up an apple and not engage. When the trend cycle made its way back around to the 'heroin chic' look of the early 1990s I didn't find myself desperate to fit into it. I felt compassion for my younger self who thought she would be rendered complete if only she could live up to its standards. The damage created by the racist, fatphobic and ableist roots of cultural beauty standards runs so deep that the effects ripple through every area of society, in ways many people are only now noticing, now that the platforms for people to share their experiences are more widespread and accessible. Social media exists outside of the traditional media outlets, meaning people don't need to make it past the gatekeepers to tell their story. It's not just thin, white women who are being platformed and held up as the ideal any more; we are exposed daily to different types of bodies. As social media overtakes many media outlets in terms of relevance, brands are having to acknowledge the demand for greater representation. Women's bodies are still treated as trends, but there are more voices than ever bravely and defiantly challenging beauty standards. This gives me hope, because it's something my teenage self wouldn't have been brave enough to dream of, never mind participate in.

I had thrown every form of hate at my body, and it survived – my heart was still beating, my lungs were still breathing – and God bless my poor liver, it was still doing its job even though it did a lifetime's work in a few years. My body wasn't the thing that made me lovable or unlovable, and it didn't take my full attention any more. It still carried a lot of pain, and I owed it the journey of processing that, so it could move comfortably in the world.

When you're used to quantifying yourself in static pictures for other people's approval, and can open an app to look at ideal versions of yourself and every single person you have ever met, it's hard to accept sometimes that your body changes, and will continue to change. Weight fluctuations are normal in sobriety, as is the ageing process (we get to do that now, and being 30 means you can't compare your skin to that of 21-year-old models). On the ever-increasing good days, I can observe, feel and appreciate my body because I think it looks absolutely fantastic, by no one else's standards other than my own. But a continued sobriety has given me the chance of making a life bigger than my body and how people view it. I can turn the voice down, challenge it and consider that my body is only one part of me.

I try never to give advice; I prefer suggestions. If you have related to anything in this section, I strongly suggest that you go to the dentist. It is an achievement, and a milestone. Lack of regard for ourselves shows up in our teeth, whether from neglecting our health, being unable to take care of ourselves or the effects of bulimia or drug use. For me it was all three. Going to the dentist is a direct and practical way to deal with the physical effects of the past, and set us up for a future where we are committed to investing the appropriate amount of care into ourselves. It's expensive, but important, especially if you're like me and have more root canals and fillings than intact teeth and are prone to abscesses. It brings up shame, pain and a whole lot of stuff you don't want to talk about – but seriously, you can do it, and you deserve it.

Starving for connection

Being teased or bullied, trying to fit in, trauma and loneliness are reasons why we try to empty or fill ourselves, to ease the ache of the missing piece. They are also the reasons why I have been terminally online since I was 13 years old.

Anorexia and bulimia can be used as terms to describe our attitudes towards being known and our relationships to other people. Emotional anorexia is a starving of the soul. It is denying yourself intimacy as a response to feeling unworthy; avoiding letting people see the part of yourself you want to hide. You put up walls, create perfectly curated avatars of yourself with a 'come closer, stay away' sign until you collapse inwards. Bulimia is a need for more, to fill a corrosive emptiness, then, from the same feeling of unworthiness, there is a fear of containing and keeping it. It is a hard and fast artificial experience of fullness; an intense, temporary connection that feels like wholeness – and though it has a short period of satisfaction, it leaves you empty, malnourished and internally devastated. They both require you to sacrifice a part of yourself. These two ways of experiencing ourselves in relation to others can show up in how we use social media. Whether we are anorexic (envious, obsessive, hyper-fixating, never showing our true self) or bulimic (losing ourselves in the need for more, more and more, and better, oversharing then feeling extreme shame, comparing and despairing), they come from the same root: I am not enough.

My friend Deborah and I related instantly over how we used the internet as adolescents. She told me: 'I was about 11 or 12, and discovered that I could lie on the internet. When strangers on MSN would ask for pics, I would use pictures of Eliza Dushku saying it was me – it felt powerful. It was a mode to step away from myself and create a fantasy identity. It represented all the things I thought I had to be, or was lacking.'

It was a convenient way to escape ourselves, forget about our issues. We could express ourselves in a way we could control by exaggerating or diminishing parts of ourselves, or literally pretending to be a different person.

'I never felt like I was right. I was never comfortable, even around my friends. I always had a tendency to get away. It started with books, then films, rewatching them, rewinding, pausing and rewinding a certain moment to get a high off it. Then on the internet, I could exist without remembering where I was. I was creating an avatar, encouraging emotional and mental joy through not living in my own reality.'

This shift from experiencing ourselves to curating ourselves happened in our personal development, and the world at large as social media took off.

'It's intentional and encouraged now with social media. You curate a version of yourself that is marketable, an idea of who you want people to see you as. Myspace was a springboard for [that] method of communication and platforming – through the curated version of "what I think I am" and "what I think people want me to be". But comparing it to other people and doing it for other people's approval fractured me from discovering who I really was. I focused, and was forced into, the version I presented, so I never asked myself who I was.'

It makes sense why we did it – to have a metric of praise and acceptance. If we get enough people to like a picture, then we'll stop feeling so awful about ourselves. If we aren't getting dopamine hits from drinking, it feels like a safer avenue to satisfy our need for more. It might mean we've made something of ourselves. You can cut, edit, delete, amplify the parts you like and lie about the parts you don't – which creates a sense of belonging, but not the experience of belonging. You never have to worry about the complexities of your whole personhood, or the vulnerability of being nuanced, because that's hard to fit into short-form, immediate content.

'I felt lonely on a soul level,' Deborah tells me, 'because I never knew who I was or felt comfortable being myself. I was so busy projecting ideas, without nurturing relationships. I lost the ability to focus on three-dimensional people. Presenting a version of yourself that is not true – that's destructive. My sense of self is challenged the most on social media, because our self-expression isn't always in line with our integrity. It's bigger than us, and scarier than us and can derail us from a true sense of self.'

When you're a grown-up sad girl and you don't want to be lonely any more

I love the internet and technology, not just in a nostalgic way for when my Tumblr was the only thing I had to worry about – I love it to this day. It has been the place where I've found friends I wouldn't have met any other way, and it allows me to always feel connected to the lives of my friends in different countries. I find events, meet-ups and causes, and learn new ways to engage with them, care about them and act on them. I have had so many moments of, 'OH, I'm not broken, because this person went through it, too, and they're a lovable human.' The identification we can find with people we never would have ordinarily crossed paths with has saved lives. The online world has created new avenues for humour, new ways to share niche interests, its own internetese language and new ways to share our experiences. On social media we can tell our stories our way, rather than have someone exploit them.

As someone who had always attempted to make sense of myself through the international, interconnected spaces on the internet, I looked towards it when I got sober. The inspirational, health-oriented recovery content online was helpful, but it wasn't meeting me where I was feeling – a feral sarcastic contrarian who was sober but still unhinged; someone who wanted to be in recovery but also wanted to complain about it.

There were a few recovery humour pages – not many, but enough to make me feel seen. I felt inspired and started memeing my day before bed, a little processing exercise to make myself laugh. It was a low-impact catharsis, to put into simple terms how everyone thought I would be a famous opera singer and

I turned into a burnt-out alcoholic, the fact that my new drug was attention from men old enough to be my father, fun contradictions like how holding my life together when I was drinking took Herculean persistence and now, sober, I was struggling to brush my teeth, and that I could survive so many things, but not two minutes in reality.

I eventually made an Instagram account, Brutal Recovery, and started posting a visual diary for myself and a few friends who were also in recovery. The unexpected brutality of being sober felt like something that just wasn't talked about much, probably because it's a less attractive pitch when promoting the road to recovery. I posted honestly, in the hope that people who were experiencing early recovery like me would know it wasn't just them, and that we weren't failing just because we were finding it hard.

With time, the follower count grew from a few thousand to over a hundred thousand, with an acceleration around the COVID lockdowns when our screens were our only resource for connection and more people than ever were directly confronted with the reality of their drinking. I kept thinking that the next thing I posted would be the thing that made me unique, but the more specific I was about my experience, the more people commented or messaged, 'Thank God, I thought I was the only one.' People shared their experiences in the comments, made suggestions and asked for help. They posted their day counts, milestones and anniversaries, signalling to whoever saw it that it's possible to struggle and stay sober; we might even laugh about it one day. It turned into a space where we could be seen and validated, for all the things we don't normally talk about when we talk about recovery. Our recovery proved we could take ourselves a bit less seriously, provided we still took our recovery more seriously than anything in our lives.

The page grew with me. Scrolling down my grid, I could see landmarks of my recovery, epiphanies I'd had, depressive periods, upswings of joy and seasons of frustration. I could see a visual testament of a life getting bigger. Things I never thought I'd get over were simply moments in time in a story that kept on going. As time passed, memes about struggling with sobriety became more reflective – something I posted after I'd privately processed the thing I was dealing with, or a retrospective of my time in early recovery, rather than how I was presently feeling. But I still posted them for the 25-year-old woman putting down her last drink now, feeling like a feral, sarcastic contrarian, and needing to be met where she's at. I started posting more of my joy as well, so she knows that it gets better, and it all belongs.

The internet was the first place where I just made sense, and even though it's different now, I'm glad it's here. I might not be sober if it wasn't for social media; it is an undeniable part of my sobriety, forever intertwined with it.

But it should get our attention that the loneliest generation is the most online. The Mental Health Foundation (MHF) reported in 2018 that 40 per cent of respondents aged 16 to 24 felt lonely often or most of the time.[3]

Like any 2005 kid, I got my parables from the internet, and on someone's Myspace profile I once read, 'Built to be lonely, to love the absent,' from the play *4.48 Psychosis* by Sarah Kane. My lonely body in that moment said, 'Oh, so that's what that is.' My dad recalls observing me as a child and telling my mum, 'I have never seen a more lonely child than Lauren.'

As a writer who needs to be alone to create, I will defend my right to be alone. I schedule my entire day around a bath, because I need time where I am entirely unobserved and unstimulated, in order to connect with myself outside of the roles I fulfil. Even now, though I have many people who I actively seek to be around for an indefinite amount of time, some of my favourite evenings are spent alone. It's not a lack of love for the people in my life, it's recognising that to be the best version of myself for those people, time by myself is a necessary and loving act. It's also a miracle that I'm able to sit with myself comfortably now.

But loneliness is different from being alone, and solitude is a different practice from isolation. These words cannot be used interchangeably as they do not mean the same thing. Being alone doesn't mean you aren't connected. Solitude and the act of being alone are a choice. Loneliness isn't; it is a symptom of separation.

Emotional loneliness is an absence of meaningful relationships, despite being surrounded by people. There is a loneliness in not being able or not feeling safe to express yourself, or in playing the role of the extroverted centre of attention to feel seen and recognised but not wanting to be perceived by anyone. Alcohol and drugs seemed to fill this gap, but between benders, when my body hummed the lament of 'lonely, lonely, lonely', I realised that bypassing the need for genuine connection wasn't the same as fulfilling it. Social loneliness is propped up by the fact that we have more resources and less time than ever, community spaces are being neglected because we are being trained to manage on our own and our energy is being consumed in a way that makes social interaction an inconvenience to the immediacy life seems to require now. When it's part of a to-do list, coffee with a friend we honestly can't live without can feel like a chore. It sometimes feels like connection has to be de-prioritised to simply keep up with everything that is being demanded of us. The demands keep increasing and socialisation is one of a million things you don't have time for – a necessary sacrifice.

And under it all is existential loneliness – a feeling of fundamental separateness from others and the wider world, the one that haunted me from when I was a child, wondering if I was a changeling. It runs like rot into the foundations of loneliness, to a disconnection from yourself, where it feels too painful or uncomfortable to be yourself around other people. Enter stage right: alcohol and drugs.

It makes you other yourself to avoid being othered by other people. It is the voice in your head that tells you no one understands you and nor do they want to. It's the barriers you put up because, God, you want to be loved but not known. The cruel thing about this type of loneliness is that there are so many people that feel it, but the condition of it is that it feels too frightening, clichéd or burdensome to share. It stops you from even wanting to know yourself.

There are higher rates of loneliness in single or widowed people and renters. With all the moving parts of the world, neighbourhoods don't function like they used to and there is a lack of social trust. Having a disability or a health condition is a huge risk factor for loneliness, as quite frankly the world is not always accessible or always understanding of people's needs. A state of loneliness is often imposed upon people if the symptoms of their mental illness are disruptive or disturbing to others.

Mental-health conditions and addiction are risk factors for loneliness. Addiction doesn't just thrive in secrecy, it thrives in the performance of 'nothing to see here – look at this, but never know me', which is the engine of social media. Getting sober can make you realise how uncomfortable it is to be yourself, and you can find yourself online being a court jester who has lost the will to live and really needs therapy (but is worried that they won't be funny any more).

There's something empowering about the fact that the people who had to do the lonely walk to the guidance counsellor's office in high school now have a place to indulgently express sadness and disorder on social media, to make it funny in the way that terrible things are funny, and to seek identification. But it can be tempting to want to be the right type of sad, to make it beautiful, digestible and meaningful. If you are open about your mental illness, you can feel the pressure of making it stylish and articulate, funny and relatable. It helps if you are waif-thin, listen to the right type of music and are doing very well.

I will always be grateful for the vulnerable, accessible and often feral parts of the internet where we can express ourselves, but part of recovery is having a place where we can experience ourselves.

Secret third thing: the third place

Traditionally, we spend our days at home and at work, with the remainder of our time being spent in 'the third place' – a term created by sociologist Ray Oldenburg.

A third place is somewhere we can be witnessed as we are, informally connect with others and eventually develop comfortable bonds. It is somewhere we choose to go regularly and feel welcome, where our presence is never required but always respected. It exists in places outside the 'cash nexus', such as parks, libraries, recreation centres, places of worship and clubs –

unfortunately, the spaces that are under threat by budget cuts and treated as unimportant by governments.

The internet is arguably becoming our third place, our devices blurring work, home and social life together. Part of me loves this, that the internet is a portal, the corners of it that we inhabit existing as something real outside of time and space, offering ever-portable access to interconnected networks that we can seamlessly move through. And yet, it doesn't always involve intimacy. Social media can be indirect; it requires no risk – we can put out riddles and signals to hope someone notices us, checking to see if the person we want to be seen by has seen it. Projecting ourselves into a grid or a timeline for people's consumption or approval doesn't make us less lonely – no more than someone looking into an aquarium makes the fish behind the glass less lonely.

A typical teenage third place is the shopping mall (not something that existed in Stranraer, but something that fascinated me as I huddled around the Morrisons fire exit). For adults, it can be the places mentioned above, and if they aren't available, bookshops, cafés, weekend markets or theatres can function as modern third places. More importantly, we can support our local libraries, parks and centres so that their validity is highlighted, and we can help protect them for the people who rely on them daily. In our era of digital loneliness, a third place helps strengthen the muscles for leaving the house, interacting with strangers, experiencing spontaneity, being perceived and being open to listening, responding and connecting (as opposed to saying things and waiting to respond with a prepared statement).

The internet is a place of gathering and connection. What's more, it is tremendously convenient. Addicts do not like inconvenience; we want to feel good, immediately. However, for a meaningful life I must occasionally be inconvenienced. My great ambition in life is to be unbothered, and I sometimes mistake that for living a life when I am never inconvenienced. It is very possible to have a life free of inconvenience – I can have everything delivered to my door immediately or the next day; I could go a whole day without getting stuck in a conversation if I don't leave the room from which I work; I can replace things rather than waiting for them to be fixed; I can get meal kits to organise how I eat without going to the supermarket; I can watch a video (on double speed) about how to do something rather than ask someone to help me.

I have to gain resilience with inconvenience and patience if I want to do favours for people, build bonds over time, show up for my friends, support small businesses and learn more about the world around me. That's the reason I wanted to continue staying sober in the first place. Friendships by nature can be inconvenient, because they require compromise, changing your plans and disrupting your routine. They require flexibility and resilience – something we need to work on in a hyper-convenient world.

I could get closer to my completely unbothered dream if I never got the Central Line again as long as I live, but it is more useful for me to endure the conditions of the Central Line (which is hell on Earth, in case you were wondering) and not be bothered by it – because at the other end is someone I love and want to spend time with.

The more I started showing up for a life outside of my phone, the more I realised that real life, and the people in it, showed up for me. It's not manipulative, it's not tit-for-tat, it's just how interpersonal relationships work. Trust and friendship building are easier when you do your part.

The tulip garden

Behavioural psychologist Marsha Linehan said in a talk at the Institute for Living in Hartford, 'If you're a tulip, don't try to be a rose. You have to find a tulip garden. All of my clients, if they're tulips, they spent all their lives trying to be roses.'

The tulip garden isn't where you fit in, it's where you belong. We all need a space where we can show up as we are, even imperfectly, and not be rejected for it. In the process, we are given the feedback that it is OK to be ourselves, and it helps us befriend ourselves in the context of befriending other people.

A community is a group of individuals with a mental and emotional involvement with each other, who are choosing to cooperate. What makes a community is how we take care of each other. I want to be in a world where people take care of each other, and if that's what I want, I have to act like it, for me and the tulips around me. Asking how we take care of ourselves and other people creates an actionable list. Learning to take care of ourselves draws out our assets and character, and indicates to us how we can take that outside of ourselves. They don't have to be anyone else's qualities. You don't have to be an organiser, a strategist and a promoter all at the same time. You can simply bring your qualities, and the community around you takes care of the rest.

Our communities, movements and relationships need us. When we're part of something, low self-esteem is challenged. If we are doing something that must be done, and contributing towards it even in the smallest way, we cannot be as useless as we can believe we are – because here we are, vital by the fact that we are simply there.

An individualistic view of healing, that it's done by ourselves and simply for ourselves, is creating lonely people (sometimes in the name of perfect boundaries, when in reality boundaries are in place for healthy and safe relationships, where conflict is inevitable but possible to tolerate and navigate. Note: this is not true in abuse dynamics or boundaries where separation or no-contact is a necessary step for continued safety). Believing that I could think my way out of loneliness turned me into a philosopher with a specialist subject of me. We can turn isolation into connection, suffering into healing and fucked-up scrap heaps of lives into second chances by realising that we are in this together, whether it's in peer-support groups, interpersonal friendships, neighbourhoods, councils, boards, workplaces, gyms or clubs. I didn't magically work out one day how to create routine, manage my impulses and veer away from sharp objects, cliff edges and walking knives – someone in my community taught me how and helped me along the way as I rewired and practised, so that I may help someone else. Being part of a community means being part of a structure. Our actions affect others. If you can't do it for yourself, remember what you're part of.

Living happily with the internet

If we are anorexic or bulimic in our social-media habits, we might have to get some boundaries on the internet. As an experiment, I tried to do two minutes of breathing before I went online. I did this for about a day, and it made me realise how much I reached for my phone every time I was a tiny bit frustrated or bored.

It made me really use my time on my phone very purposefully, because the cost of entry was two minutes of deep focus. It made me think about my motives. Maybe entering the internet sphere with a large awareness of my breath and body made me fully aware that when I was doom scrolling, whether it was an ex's social media, all the things I'll never own or more and more details on tragic news, I was emotionally cutting. When I find myself automatically seeking negative reactions, I ask myself to slow down, really wonder what I'm doing and why I'm doing it. I want to know about the things happening in the world, because I want to be a part of them. However, seeking the worst, most terrible news about it in order to feel more terrible isn't fulfilling that desire. I must extend to the outside world, taking action where I can, and generally moving more slowly and purposefully.

Anyone who has had the Sunday-afternoon notification that their screentime was seven hours this week has lamented over the 'better things they could be doing'. If we want to be doing 'better' things, we have to be intentional with them. There are already too many things to do, so we have to be specific. Write down one or two things that you would rather be doing than being on your phone, and when you reach for it to feel a comfortable weight in your palm, train yourself to ask, 'Do I want my phone, or do I want to do this other thing?' Maybe sometimes you do want your phone – sometimes we want to zone out if we are overstimulated, and if we go in with that awareness, we are intentional with what we want out of it.

Jenny Odell examined the internet carefully in *How to Do Nothing* (2019), a book about resisting the 'attention economy' – originally a term used to describe the problem of information overload as an economic one, now more commonly used to describe our attention as the limiting factor in the consumption of information. Digital data roughly doubles every two years, which makes human attention a valuable commodity that everything online is trying to gain.

Odell doesn't argue that we despair, ignore or give in to the idea that the internet is making us lonely, distracted and superficial – but refuses the idea that we're productivity machines built to be used. She encourages us to redirect our attention to the present moment, listening, connecting and detangling the ways our identities are trapped in work or online presence, so we can think less about personal brand and corporate values, and more about personal values.

She says: 'My only real interest in technology was how it could give us more access to physical reality, which is where my real loyalties were.'

Social media feels healthy for me when my world outside is bursting with life, and what spills over goes into my social media.

I have seen the internet rendered most powerfully when it was used as a platform to help people gather, organise, create and attend events, to make things accessible, and to involve and acknowledge people who are falling off.

The internet gave me my first sense of wonder; it was the thing that was bigger than myself. It was a place where I could see beyond, to a bigger life, which was an absolute lifeline for a kid who didn't fit in. Part of my growing up and growing braver was actively seeking that out in the wider world, and making it real. The fascination meets bravery, and your world gets even bigger.

IX. When Things Get Hard

BoJack: Life's a bitch and then you die, right?
Diane: Sometimes. Sometimes life's a bitch and then you keep living.

— *BoJack Horseman*

When you get sober for everything to be OK and it isn't. When you didn't get sober for THIS. When things feel out of control but you're sober this time.

In 2020 I was two years sober, and I had finally created a career I could write home about after spending the last eight years studying while trying to launch as a young artist, begging for scholarships and sacrificing most of my sanity. During this time I was performing, while doing admin for a church, cleaning for Airbnb, teaching undergraduate voice, preparing the subtitles for operas I wasn't in, working as an assistant for an operations manager and ushering at a concert hall.

I reached the point where it had all become worth it. I had

Mahler symphonies 4 and 8 on the books, *La Traviata* to prepare for and agents wanted to meet with me in New York City to discuss representation. As a woman in the arts from a rural working-class background who had given up so much to be here, with so many setbacks, I felt like I'd proved myself and given my sobriety legitimacy. I was no longer almost losing my job in a department store for being sick on a customer when I was hungover (in my defence, it was New Year's Day – who returns a hoover on New Year's Day?) and being sent home because the manager said I looked like I was 'dragged out of the sea'. I was a full-time opera singer on the East Coast of America, finally a sobriety success story. Then I got an unusual text saying I wasn't allowed to leave my house, and, well, we all know what happened after that.

I wilfully believed COVID wouldn't cancel my performances, because it couldn't be happening to me – my dreams were about to come true. It had to work out. Opera houses were closed, performances were delayed then cancelled, agents weren't taking on new clients any more and my naive thinking started to catch up with reality. But there was someone to depend on in all this: Dominic. When certainty is taken away we are presented with what we can't ignore. In this situation it was that he was American, and I was on a visa. Though my temperament slotted neatly into the northeastern states, socially I was always the girl with the funny accent – and bureaucratically I was a non-resident alien who could be taken away at a moment's notice. Visas are often a make-or-break issue for international couples, and at this moment, under these conditions, I couldn't get one. I was going to have to leave the country where we met and were building a life together.

There were many nights of sitting in quietness, neither of us wanting to ignore reality, but also not wanting to talk about it – because there were no answers or proof that anything would be OK. Eventually we made a plan to move to London together – while I couldn't get a visa for the USA, he could get one for the UK. In the plan I trusted, even though I did not have a job, only knew one person in London and had no idea what I was going to do when I got there, especially because singing in public was literally illegal. I had a vague desire to live there, like any dreamer who looked at New York City skylines or Hollywood-sign pictures and thought, *I want something bigger*, and London fitted that, so it was something to work with. I was going to miss the mint-green, colonial-style house my flat was in, my reading armchair on the peeling front porch, the sights of my early recovery milestones, CVS pharmacies and the feeling of being foreign and interesting to the people around me. I was going to miss New Haven, the place where I'd turned a disaster into a new life, with drip coffee makers, Polar Seltzer and Hot Pockets (my faithful accompaniment to the achingly long nights of my early recovery). Most of all I'd miss the people, like Nora, my first close friend in recovery. We kept seeing each other at meetings, registering that we were the same age, and she eventually approached me saying, 'I think we should be friends.' Her, and her directness, were thrilling to be around and her boldness emboldened me, opening me up to the rest of the group. In my last week in New Haven the women I got sober with organised a picnic in East Rock Park to say goodbye. I was given a silver bracelet with 'Keep Fucking Going' engraved inside it, and I went home to pack my entire life into two suitcases. I was going to miss this chapter, because I thought it was going to be where the story happened.

But I had Dominic, someone who had never once let me down, who loved me unconditionally, consistently, even when I felt I didn't deserve it. We had talked about marriage sleepily on my birthday that year in bed after dinner, our hair and hands tangled. This was a change to the plan, but I thought it would make us stronger – and maybe we could return to America when the world had sorted itself out. I would become a citizen and we'd think of it as our year abroad.

The break-up happened two months after we moved into our one-bedroom flat in Tower Hamlets.

The weird thing about heartbreak is what our mind protects us from, and what it won't let us forget. I don't remember how I started the conversation that acknowledged we didn't know how to love each other any more and ended with the decision to stop trying, but I do remember picking up oven pizzas for dinner, because I didn't know how much effort you should put into an 'I-think-we-should-break-up' meal. I remember realising that I was wearing a T-shirt I loved, and I would never be able to wear it again without thinking of this moment. I don't remember what he said when I said, 'I can't do this any more,' but I remember him saying, 'Thank you for being the brave one.' When we're drinking, our brain can blackout to protect us from remembering the horrors we couldn't handle sober. So it is for getting kicked out of a pub for re-enacting a scene from *Rent* on a table, so it is for the moment you decide that two and a half years of doing your best just isn't working.

Like Ernest Hemingway described bankruptcy, everything crumbled, 'Gradually, then suddenly.' I went from a full schedule, a relationship I thought would never end and living in a place where I couldn't leave the house without bumping into at least three people I knew, to applying for Universal Credit, being a stranger to everyone in my neighbourhood and single. I had lost my career's big break, everywhere around me people were dying and my body was physically aching with loneliness. I had spent two years lovingly trying to know my mum, rather than being an emotionally absent city-daughter, and now I couldn't get on a train to give her a hug. I didn't really know UK culture any more, having been away for five years, and thought I'd never have to engage with it again after making a big escape to America. I met people from Zoom meet-ups for socially distanced walks with 'Hi, I'm Lauren, I'm totally fine, very normal and funny, but the fabric of my life is in shreds – also, what's a flat white? No, I haven't watched *Line of Duty*, and do they not sell ten-packs or menthols any more?'

Heartbreak

In the immediate aftermath I, miraculously, didn't want to drink. I also didn't want to eat, sleep or talk to anyone – but something inside me wanted to survive this. Some days I was numb, and others I couldn't touch a surface without leaving a smudge of wet mascara and liquid eyeliner on it. It was like early recovery again; sometimes the bigger things felt easier than the small things. I exercised more than I ever had in my life but couldn't make a meal (what a time to find out you have low blood pressure). I got a job teaching piano on Zoom, but the effort it took to go to work (literally sitting on a computer in my living room) left me with no energy for anything else. I could send a text but not reply to one.

I was very good at telling people I was doing things I wasn't actually doing. I loved telling people I was being very gentle with myself and mourning what I had lost, while doing nothing of the sort. It got me through the initial shock, and it worked up to the point where I realised I wasn't dealing with the break-up; I was too busy trying to convince everyone how well I was doing. In many ways I was doing well – I was not drunk. In many ways I was tormenting myself by trying to outsmart and outrun grief.

I was swiping on a dating app when it hit me: as much as he had left my life for the right reasons, I'd once loved him, and the future we had was no longer one I'd walk into. Parts of myself that were enmeshed with him were hanging off as unfinished amputations and un-cauterised wounds. I would literally never be the same ever again. The person I was when we started dating didn't exist any more, and I had about a hundred little mannerisms, language twists and new interests because of him. I felt full of false borrowed traits that weren't mine. Maybe I was just a jangling mess of all the people I have dated and nothing more. I panicked, and wanted him back because our incomplete arc was going to be with me forever anyway. I wondered if this was all just a horrible mistake.

I needed to get out of the flat we once shared, so I went to dissociate in ASDA for a little bit. I needed turkey mince, anyway. Dominic always took care of the food shopping; I didn't know where anything was in the aisles. I didn't even like turkey mince, I just ate it because he liked it. Confusion turned into panic. I wanted to just look at the bottles in the booze aisle, maybe hold one in my hand. My brain was dizzy with the possibility of escaping this. 'After all, this is what alcohol is for,' it told me, convincingly. Before I turned this feeling into a fact, I called my friend Max. I said I knew I couldn't drink but there was something big and terrible inside me and I didn't know what to do, and I needed him to tell me what a bad sober person I was, how weak and undisciplined I was. He said: 'You're in hell with no map or blueprint. Of course you want to drink.'

I was finally ready to be honest. I don't think I was being dishonest before. I just wasn't ready to go there just yet. I told him how heartbroken I was, how much I regretted, how I was scared I'd ruined my chance at love. How I hated turkey mince and had all along, but I was going to miss eating it. I finally felt ready to let people into the pain, and have them help me hold it together even for a ten-minute phone conversation. I was done pretending there was nothing to see here, deceiving myself and others that I was a picture of togetherness.

I sat in the bath for hours that night with a Red Bull and a box of Milk Tray, saying, 'I did not get sober for this, I did not get sober for this.'

Crying out the Ho'oponopono prayer and asking the universe for a fucking sign and not another lesson, I asked myself why I even bothered getting sober to be in this much pain, and some wise part of my brain recognised that this was exactly what I got sober for. I got sober to handle life as it happened, and make more loving choices. I got sober to react differently to life, especially when it was hard. I got sober to change, and here was an opportunity to practise. Sobriety wasn't making life painful; pain exists as a fact of life. Sobriety wasn't doing these things to me, this was just life happening, and sometimes it doesn't happen the way you want it to.

If shitty things happening were an excuse to drink, every sober person would be drunk right now. If I needed perfect circumstances to get or stay sober, I would never have got there. It is not a question of how strong I am – I can be as strong as I'll ever be and still not be able to control the uncontrollable. The strongest things I've ever done were when I allowed things to be taken out of my hands when they needed to be, maybe before I felt ready, and dealt with what that brought up in me. The strongest things I did in this period were calling friends and saying, 'I need help.' Saying yes to a dinner invitation when I wanted to stay in and feel sorry for myself. Deciding to change my cookware because I wanted to start cooking for myself again after I lost my appetite for weeks. It was sending off job applications, and spending a night writing and eating chocolate buttons by candlelight to start processing the emotional gulf that the recently ended relationship had left inside me.

I was in the middle space of not knowing what was to come, but finally ready to start letting go of what was behind me. I was frustrated going forward, working for something with an unknown outcome, but in the process I realised that we never know what we're working towards. I was in uncharted waters, learning to embrace the mystery and hating every second of it. But still, if I could be so fascinated by the mystery of the world, mythology, poetry and history, perhaps I could be that interested and accepting of the unknown in my own life. I didn't have to throw it away just because I didn't know where I was going – I never really had, and I'd got this far.

After months of paying lip service to 'it is for the best' and taking care of myself even when I didn't want to, one day I looked up at the map on the Northern Line, between Old Street and Moorgate, and I realised that the pain of losing a life I thought I'd live didn't have an ice grip on me any more. It had travelled from the head to the heart, and now something that had been taking up an enormous amount of space with its ache just wasn't there. Maybe it was time, maybe it was grace, maybe it was because there was more in my life now than the loss. It was worth staying sober through the restoration process for that realisation – that quiet moment of knowing that things aren't always OK, but I could be. A lot of the time things eventually will be OK, but they might be different. Sometimes you have to let your heart break, so it can fall back into place.

Death and loss

Sometimes we lose something that can't be replaced, and we can't apply the 'it's-all-working-out-for-the-highest-good' salve that we would for a break-up, a job loss or an old idea about yourself.

I went home to Scotland for my first sober Christmas in 2018, when I was less than a year sober. I had done everything I could to prepare myself for the weight of feeling the entire population saturated with December stress, tight-jawed, broke and exhausted, and for being an adult in my childhood bedroom, with the onslaught of emotion that provokes at a time of year when it's acceptable to drink at any time of day. My community waited anxiously for me to return, hopefully sober, to ask me how it went. I told them it was great, except my grandmother died.

We had been losing my grandmother for a long time to dementia, tugged with the tide of the moments of lucidity when she would remember my face and name, and we would sing Scottish folk songs together. I was drunk for many of these moments – we were two people talking around the edges of our minds' black holes, but still loving each other from somewhere certain inside.

I couldn't work out if her death made it harder or easier not to think about drinking. On the one hand, I had to deal with complex emotions that would have been so much easier to eradicate. On the other, all the things I thought were issues and problems that really mattered now didn't. I had just held my grandmother's hand and sung to her on her last day on Earth. I had been brought into reality with something that reminded me how much I needed to live while I had the chance.

I got to play the piano at her funeral, stand by her grave and cry, share and listen to everyone's memories, because I was sober. I chose her painting of the Ailsa Craig, a volcanic plug in the middle of the Irish Sea, as my heirloom. It was excruciating to feel these things when under a year sober, but I knew what she would do in the face of confusion or pain: she would make some pancakes, do something helpful and remind me of the importance of family – a family I was now getting much closer to because I was sober. Working on my recovery was helping me remember who I was, and one of those things was her granddaughter. When things felt complicated, I was simply grateful she existed, and the love she gave me when she said, 'You'll be all right in your time,' exists in me, to spread to other people.

Being present for this grief brought up more than I'd bargained for. I was 18 when I experienced my first major loss. Alastair and I met when I was 16, at a One Act Play Festival, during my most socially awkward, lonely high-school years, when I ate my lunch in the bathroom or my English teacher's classroom. He was standing in the aisles of the theatre during a break, and something told me to talk to him; something made me sit on the stairs with him and do the same thing the day after for the next few weeks. He was the first person to be kind to me in a very long time. Over the months we got to know each other, I started soft-launching my actual personality, gradually allowing myself to be known by someone. I stopped being scared of having opinions, favourite films and ideas. Most people thought aspiring to become an opera singer was weird, but he said he would be in the front row when I made my debut, and I considered that maybe the world wasn't such a hostile place after all. Every time we were together I kept expecting it to be the day he realised I was selfish, rotten and broken, but instead we just made plans: to go to the Proms, to help out at a fundraiser together, that he would come see me at the hotel where I played the piano. A week before we were going to see Belle and Sebastian in Glasgow, I sent the last text he would ever read from me: 'I'll see you when we're both home.'

I had let my phone die in the middle of the night and didn't expect that when I charged it, between a morning shift in the department store and a recording for a Christmas concert broadcast, that everything would change. He was killed instantly in a freak accident on his drive home, on the road that overlooked the Ailsa Craig. You don't switch on your phone and expect your entire relationship to the universe and its laws to change now that something so awful, so unexpected and so unlikely to happen has happened.

Words didn't exist in this new universe where he didn't exist any more. I felt stranded, still screaming when there was nothing left in my lungs. I couldn't do this now, I thought, I had to be on-stage in three hours, and I don't remember anything else from the day. Blank, blackout, my brain protecting itself. I woke up the next morning, after a dream that someone had died, thinking how awful it would be, to die around Christmas. Then I remembered: someone I loved *had* died, and I was going to have to work out how to live with that. I became a morning drinker.

I dealt with this loss for the first time when I got sober, eight years after his death. It unexpectedly ruptured from somewhere inside me like an oil slick, changing my ecosystem by blackening everything it touched and making what once looked like stable ground unsafe to walk on.

Returning to somewhere you've never been before

Living with grief can be framed like any type of recovery – it's an ongoing process. You are finding your way back to yourself after you have been irreversibly changed. There's a version of yourself you knew before and the one you know now, and neither of them feels like you for an uncertain amount of time. When you experience grief young you're already in the uncertain disorientation of discovering who you are, and you don't have certain social, personal, financial or professional securities to anchor you. You're left rudderless, having to believe that, with time, what initially feels like a broken piece becomes a part of your existence in a way that doesn't always hurt.

Whether the grief is historic or immediate, whether it has torn you open or numbed you into the desolation of even your feelings being lost to you, or it's an abrupt drag into what you are truly feeling, it isn't a feeling. Like recovery, it's an experience with no timeline that requires self-acceptance, compassion and patience, and most people think they're doing it wrong.

Anne Lamott describes the process in her book *Plan B: Further Thoughts on Faith* (2004):

> If you haven't already, you will lose someone you can't live without, and your heart will be badly broken, and you never completely get over the loss of a deeply beloved person. But this is also good news. The person lives forever, in your broken heart that doesn't seal back up. And you come through, and you learn to dance with the banged-up heart.

The confusion, longing, distress and hollowness of significant loss is something we can only consolidate for ourselves, but it doesn't have to be a solo journey. The separation anxiety of losing something huge finds solace in connectivity. Like addiction, grief can be bigger than us, and doesn't need to be handled as an individual burden. When something that once felt like love turns into an absence so painful it makes you doubt everything about your existence, the love and support of other people helps the unwelcome space find its new shape. Even if they aren't feeling the magnitude of what you are feeling, a dependable person can help pave the way for the next steps, and remind us why we choose recovery even when we feel like it's pointless in a world that's become uncertain.

Grief needs a safe container, which can be found in community. Community never requires you to show up perfectly, which is necessary because grief can be imperfect, messy, spiky, rude, anti-social, stubborn and afraid. With fellow grievers we can get that feeling that we craved in childhood – the 'it-is-OK-that-you-feel-like-this' reassurance. Sharing the rage, despair and hopelessness with fellow grievers creates trust, which makes a safe place for laughter, identification and everything else in the picture – the life that keeps going.

If you live with or around addiction, not all of your friends make it out alive, which creates an odd survivor's guilt around who gets to stay and who gets taken.

I had a friend in recovery who would sneak me into his gym when I couldn't afford a membership but wanted to lift heavy things to get through some early sobriety overwhelm. He gave me rides to the supermarket because he knew I didn't have a car and made many other gestures that on the surface may not seem remarkable but changed everything more than he'll ever know. He relapsed and died in 2020. I'm not living for him today, as his life was his own, but I let his actions ripple through me. The grief of loss may have changed me irreversibly, but I was equally changed by his kindness, and that change can help me make tiny changes where I can, just like he did. I tell the stories of my friends who didn't make it, not as sensational tales or anecdotes, but to honour the humans they were. I love and continue to love them, even if I'm scared that one day I'll forget the sound of their voice.

Sometimes you have to accept that you will spend the rest of your life missing someone, and it gets easier but doesn't ease the missing of them. To be sober and grieve is to feel everything, and I choose to feel it, because even though it doesn't always offer me comfort, it's often said that grief is love with nowhere to go, and a grieving world needs my love.

When I booked tickets for my first rave in sobriety, after being too much of a homebody for too long, I thought I was anxious until I realised that the twitch in my ribcage was actually excitement. I remembered how Alastair always told me that you will enjoy your life more if you always have something you're excited about locked in as a concrete plan – doesn't matter if it's a day, a week or a month away. I don't think it's something I would have taken as seriously if the loss of him didn't make me realise how important it was. I wish I didn't have to lose him to realise it, but it makes me listen to people more intently now – because we shouldn't only take their words as life-changing because they died young.

When I performed Tatyana in *Eugene Onegin* in 2019 – the first major role I performed sober – I bought him a ticket in the front row. It didn't bring him back, but it made me feel better.

The issue with control

It's natural to want to numb out the earth-shattering, self-conception-rupturing things that happen outside of our control – there were times in our life when they were threats to our existence. Even when we aren't in immediate danger, they are a reminder that terrible things can happen – these involuntary reality checks shake the illusion of certainty. What little trust we might have in a benevolent, or even benign, universe disappears. In this wound, where the past bleeds through into the present moment, we want to reach for temporary relief and grasp for control. Any other option feels like letting our guard down as the world as we know it crumbles. We have entered a realm where we have realised how little control we have, and how painful that can be.

We'll do anything for an illusion of control: we catastrophise, project, develop a fourteen-step skincare routine, get into a new relationship, move into the gym, isolate, drink, do drugs, worry, ruminate — anything that makes us feel like we are the masters of our destiny: *I can't control the horrors, but I can control this.*

I once stood awkwardly in the middle of a hula hoop, as a mindfulness teacher told me that everything in the hula hoop was what I had control over right then. She told me the sky might fall, and all we would be able to control was our reaction to it. I bristled, wondering why she immediately grabbed for the improbable 'the sky is falling', not brave enough to say something specific like, 'Someone you love has been killed in a car crash, and all you have to control is what's in your hula hoop.' I supposed I didn't have to take it so literally. Everyone's sky falls at some point, whether it's a car crash, a diagnosis, a disappointment or a death. Maybe it was good we were in the sky, because she asked me to look at the clouds, see how they were moving. That's everything, she said. They were big simplifications, but when things are complicated sometimes it's good to reach for something simple.

She taught us about radical acceptance, for the circumstances when there is an undeniable problem, which is undeniably unfair, but we don't want to turn our pain into suffering. We can observe the pain and acknowledge disappointment, frustration and grief — and still move forward. Between acceptance and action is where we get our choices. The greatest example of radical acceptance was demonstrated to me in my childhood, when my family's entire flock of sheep was culled to stop the spread of foot and mouth disease in 2001. We had a map and protractor on our kitchen table, mapping out the 2km cull. When we fell into the perimeter, something that we never thought would happen was happening. I watched my parents grieve their entire livelihood, powerless as their life's work was taken away from them. And they started again, with a new breed of sheep that eventually brought them greater success; they kept going, simply because that was what they had to do. They didn't have to approve of the disease, they didn't have to enjoy it, but they didn't fight the reality of it – and they moved on, doing what had to be done.

When I told my therapist in 2020 that I was so tired of all the gradual work I had to do to navigate this period of my life, she brought up radical acceptance again, but with an analogy. She told me to imagine I was in jail. She asked me, do I sit in my jail cell and cry about the situation (I can if I like; it would be really understandable given the circumstances) or do I find whatever energy I have, even if it's only enough to wiggle my big toe, and get ripped in the gym, read everything in the library, work on my case and what my options will be once I get out? I told her, I'd probably want to cry for a bit – then get into the library.

Most people have a passing knowledge of the serenity prayer – the serenity to accept the things I cannot change, the courage to change the things I can and the wisdom to know the difference. It's not just something that was said because there was nothing else on offer, or because it looks cute embroidered on pillows – it's a set of instructions for how to manage the shit we can and can't change and work out exactly where those lines are drawn. 'The wisdom to know the difference' means that we do not have to accept the thing we can change, and there are things we can do to change the things we can't accept, we just have to be mindful of what those things really are.

Accepting what you cannot control leaves space to focus your efforts, and changing what you can shows you that the situation is not as hopeless as you imagine, and despite it all you are still here. Recovery can often throw you in the deep end of your life. Continuing in the face of challenging times reminds you that though you can be gentle, you are not fragile. I thought I had to be 'in control' of every situation, create perfect conditions, to remain stable and secure, but recovery is remaining adjusted to life when everything around me was an unmitigated disaster. At least fewer and fewer of these situations were my fault any more.

In the immediate aftermath of losing something you thought you couldn't live without, doing loving acts for yourself feels pointless, but it's the most vital time to form pathways and remain open as the time takes the time it takes. This compassion is necessary when you face yourself, see what you've lost, what you want back, parts you gained from the experience and are grateful for, and things that don't fit any more. A broken heart needs patience. It is the process of what is yours returning to you, and what isn't yours going back to where it belongs. It can be painful, but it's a pain that can change you for the better.

What we can depend on is that things will change, and to allow that we must keep going. Faith can be just taking the next step. If we don't have faith that things can change, we can have faith in ourselves that we will commit to doing what must be done, remembering that something has ruptured and that we have to go easy.

PART IV

*The final frontiers are often said to be romance and finance.
I have nothing to offer on the latter, but I have some experience
of the former – how to navigate sex, love and dating
with all the wounds that they aggravate.*

X. Sex and Love

I stopped using marijuana.
It was using up all of my imagination.
Drinking became boring.
But sex never let me down.
    – David Keenan, *This Memorial Device* (2017)

When all you ever wanted was to be loved, and you got a little bit lost along the way. When you want to be loved, but are scared of what that means. When the thought of getting vulnerable in front of someone sober makes you want to tear your skin off.

It was early 2021, I was almost three years sober and on the phone to Nicholas. He heard me sliding a dress over my legs and hooking the straps over my shoulders. I was trying to be inconspicuous, but Nicholas isn't the sort of person you can get things past.

'Where are you going?' he asked.
'To bed,' I lied.

In about six hours I'd be on an emotional comedown, lonely and wondering, again, why I'm enough to be wanted but too much to love. But I never thought that far ahead when I was getting ready; I was thinking of how intoxicating it was to get a text from someone who wanted only me, the cattle-prod jolt of anticipation when I sent my ETA in the Uber, and how for the next few hours I didn't have to think about anything else. Self-hatred disintegrated in the unique effort someone puts in when they are trying to have sex with you, if only for the period they're desiring you. Maybe this time would be different, and I wouldn't feel that confusing emptiness that comes after you get what you thought you wanted and it doesn't change who you are.

'I'm going to see Liam,' I admitted.

'I'd rather you were going to see Jack the Ripper,' Nicholas replied.

'I'm wearing green – should I go with black instead?' I say, deflecting.

'You should go to *church*.'

'Yeah, I'm going to go with black.'

'An appropriate choice for your emotional crucifixion.'

He'd heard altogether too much about Liam, and had absolutely had it with me by this point.

Liam had made it very clear he didn't have what I wanted him to give, but I'd sometimes pretend we were a normal, real couple in the few minutes after hooking up – when we held each other briefly, or lay back breathless and holding hands, before we rolled over and checked our phones. I always said no when he offered to pay for the Uber back; I didn't need him – but still secretly wished if I was just good enough, or caught him on the right day, he would see something lovable in me and ask to do something in public, with clothes on, sometime.

I was almost three years sober and looking for a drink with legs. I mean, at least I wasn't getting drunk. I'd go to tragic lengths to try to get people who didn't see me as human to want to be with me. Usually, it involved having sex with them, hoping they'd fall in love with me and slicing off a part of myself — usually the part of myself that needed what they couldn't give me. When I wasn't seeing Liam, I was finding freelance creatives, preferably twenty years older than me, to assign magical qualities to. We would have five-hour phone calls, sharing in rhapsody how amazing it was that we'd found each other and making big plans for our shared future. Around the six-week mark of these high-intensity, low-reality relationships, the messages would become shorter and less frequent, and there would be another ghost in the graveyard of my WhatsApp archived folder.

I loved a photographer — you know, because they'll see me. If I had a dollar for every man I dated who had a shrine to Jim Morrison, I would have two dollars, which isn't a lot, but it's too many. I wanted someone who was a little tortured and stuck in the past. Nothing thrilled me like a divorce in their history, to be told I'm so different from their ex, until eventually it transpired that we're exactly the same person a decade apart. I would make myself convenient, without needs, so long as they just kept giving me the bare minimum to appease my feeling of worthlessness. I would wait for enough crumbs so that I could push them together into a cake.

After someone I had been on two dates with abruptly stopped talking to me, I found myself catatonic on my couch. I thought this was the one; we had the same tattoo and he said his cat really liked me. I'd assigned him the role of curing what I felt was fundamentally broken about me by showing me I was worthy of love, and like the rest of the people I'd put that unreasonable demand on, he revealed himself to be human.

On my third day of immobilising depression, surrounded by Tesco Meal Deals and more disposable vapes than I care to admit, I read *The Pisces* (2018) by Melissa Broder – where a woman, fresh from a break-up and uninspired by her work, falls in love with a mysterious swimmer who turns out to be a merman. Her obsession runs so deep she abandons everything else in her life, and almost drowns to be with him. Despite the fact that Broder was describing having sex with a literal merman, I had never related to a book more. Especially when she said, 'I believe in love more than anything. But I think I am very bad at it.' I called Nora to tell her about this man ghosting me after seeming so into me, reading her our text threads, telling her the dates, times and lengths of all our phone calls, asking her what I had done wrong. She listened kindly, then said, with her classic directness, 'Is this not getting boring for you?' She was right. This pattern was not only harming me, but was becoming so fucking boring.

I'm a girl who loves things

There is something in my heart that has a high sensitivity to fascination. It is always open for the next thing that's going to steal its imagination and let new passions rush in. I do not just like things, I love them. I have always been a romantic, I sent my first love letter when I was seven. Using stickers from a magazine as stamps, I described to him the cataclysm he had created inside me, how I wanted to devote myself to him. In music class he licked the top of his recorder and passed it to me, as a kiss. That recorder had a lot to answer for, because from that point on, I was desperate for anything that tasted like love. My first boyfriend – a drummer in a metal band – initiated me into this new world where I felt like love could choose you, and deliver happiness to you. Even after it ended and I had my first heartbreak, I was now feeling the slightly delicious hyperbolic agony of heartache.

There's a musicians' parable where a student asks his teacher, 'Why do we do this horrible, unstable, exhausting career built on the sacrifice of our sanity?' and the teacher replies, 'Because we want to be loved.' In music and drama school, I was in a group of people who were so love-hungry we became performers to make the giving and receiving of love between performer and audience our job. It was an instant hit of the far-off dream of 'life might have something better for me', 'all this feeling has meaning' and 'if I am good enough, I will be loved'. In a role, you could give so much of yourself and get an acknowledgement of worthiness, though your heart knows the difference between attention and being truly seen and loved, even if you don't.

Love meant that I mattered enough to be cared about. I wanted to matter, so I wanted to be in love. But my obsession with love developed a life of its own – it was a heat-seeking missile. It made me selfish, volatile and demanding, unable to see people for who they were other than the person who was going to rescue me. My drinking added a detonator to these relationships, where inevitably we'd end up screaming at each other in the street, before I would back down and beg them not to leave me.

I craved the attention of men; there was no other way I knew how to feel good about myself, and no amount of it would be enough. When a work-fling broke up with me at a train station I wanted to push him onto the track, unable to handle this betrayal of my expectation on him to make me feel OK. It flicked through my mind as something I genuinely had to convince myself not to do. The thrill of new love was getting less and less every time, but I couldn't stop. There was something inside me I was trying to make right by being loved, and if it made me selfish, volatile and demanding, then I thought I must just be those things. I stopped caring that men sensed my desperation and saw it as an opportunity to use me, because I was using them – I was beating them to the punch this time.

If I am loved, it will make up for everything

I could acknowledge that sexual abuse was real, but I had a self-blaming narrative of: 'It happens to sweet, innocent girls and not difficult, alcoholic bitches like me. What I got was only what I deserved – I am a handful.' We often use self-blame to make sense of abuse, neglect or tragedy we have no control over – thinking it was caused by something inherently bad about us seems to have more order than 'something bad happened, and I don't understand why'.

He had parked at the top of the winding road that ran up to my house, far from where anyone could see us. He was stroking my arm as I sat silently, belted in the passenger seat. When he dropped me off, I sprinted up the stairs to my room and got his touch off me by shredding my skin with my fingernails. I rubbed until the skin broke away in bundles, like a pilled cardigan. I didn't even remember what I was forgetting. I told myself the worst thing was him stroking my arm, telling me how special and beautiful I was. I'd become very good at forgetting; it kept getting easier. He didn't start with the abuse; he started by making sure I needed him. When I did things right he told me that I was an unusual talent, something extraordinary to find. When he wasn't happy with me his critiques became insults; he pointed out things that were broken about me. I would have done anything to please him. I was 13, he was a tutor, and he said he could make me a star.

One day he handed me a sheet of paper with phone numbers on it, telling me it was a list of new tutors to contact, because he couldn't work with me any more. He told me my bad attitude was irreparable, and that he needed someone who was willing to do whatever it takes to be successful. I cried and told him how scared, insecure and sorry I was. He looked satisfied and took the sheet of paper from my hands and put it in the bin. That's when I remember the abuse starting. Except I wouldn't call it that for many years. I'd just keep pushing it down – it was my fault, after all.

I was still this child years later when a boyfriend in Glasgow vetted my friends and convinced me of hateful things they said behind my back, to encourage me to cut them off. He told me I hung the moon, then that I was incapable, pathetic and fragile, but never too fragile to handle his rage when I broke his ever-movable set of imaginary rules, like speaking to the wrong person, not having sex when he wanted it or having a journal. I kept trying to win his game until I was convinced I deserved it, and being called a lying slut became a normal Tuesday morning. This was just the cost of entry for being loved, I thought. Aside from all that, he could be so loving, and I had a pattern of mistaking control for care.

I was still this child in my last week in Bloomington, Indiana, when I woke up next to a man I did not know. Convinced he was asleep or dead, I went to the kitchen, where all my plates were smashed on the floor. I found my phone between the couch cushions, the screen cracked down the middle, and $100 worth of cheese from the Kroger store in my fridge. I remembered a dive bar, and trying to shake him by telling him I needed to go grocery shopping. I remembered him following me, and I pretended to fill my basket with things so he would leave me alone. I must have resigned myself to sleeping with him somewhere between the cheese aisle and the checkout. The memory-zaps started – I just wanted him out of my house. He said my choices were that I give him money for a taxi or fuck him. I honestly didn't consider my body to be worth as much as the $20 I needed to spend on vodka to forget this. There wasn't any guarantee that it would have got him to leave anyway. I drank the rest of the wine on top of my fridge and let him have sex with me over the kitchen table. After he was done, he asked me if I finished. I said yes and he punched the back of my head, calling me a liar. I caught myself in the reflection of the kettle. I had scratches all over my face and collarbone. I rolled my eyes at myself, thinking, *Again?* and wondered whether to go to Chipotle later. 'It's not anything anyone hasn't done to me before,' I told myself, 'there's nothing anyone can do to hurt me now.'

I was still the same girl who wrote love letters, offering my heart as the most precious thing I had. I was just a girl who wanted to be loved and to love someone.

As I continued to thaw out emotionally, I realised this wasn't someone in a bleak short story I was working on – it was me. It was my history, and even though I wasn't in any abusive dynamics any more, it crept up on me, like when I was getting a massage and thought, *It's happening again, don't move, it will be over soon*, as it travelled to my legs, or when a doctor put a speculum inside me and my instinct was to grind back and pretend to enjoy it, or when I cried at the nail salon, because a man was holding my hand in a non-sexual way.

I also wasn't sure whether I was in love with every hot dad, my exes and anyone who was nice to me, or if I'd never been in love before.

Chasing love means you never have to sit still long enough to risk intimacy

The ease, comfort and sense of fullness I was looking to extract from alcohol and drugs was a longing for love – one where I didn't have to be emotionally vulnerable. It made sense; I'd been vulnerable before, and look what happened.

It's not inherently malicious to want to be loved, but it can be tricky territory when a text back from the right person can feel like ecstasy and you're a drug addict. Or if you just wanted to be loved and got used and abused along the way, which has left you with more than a few crossed wires. What doesn't kill you makes you very uncomfortable experiencing intimacy. Rather than letting someone in close enough to hurt you, you might want a narrative of love, putting each other on pedestals and working more on the idealised versions of each other than the actual relationship. You might want to be entirely self-sufficient – because you've been let down in the past and you want to believe that you need no one and nothing. You might want to protect your heart, because no one protected you before, by abandoning before you are abandoned. There are a million ways you can avoid intimacy, like dating emotionally withholding people (no, I AM especially mature and different, I'll be the one to win their love), conducting text relationships (an idealised person who lived in my phone and my imagination) and pursuing other people's boyfriends (if you're scared of intimacy, you will never run the risk of getting too close to someone if you date someone you will never, ever be able to get too close to).

This is not exclusive to romantic partners. This fear can be in platonic relationships, throughout families and towards humanity as a whole. Human relationships are uncertain by nature. It's hard to accept that in truly loving someone there's a 100 per cent chance that at some point you will get hurt. They are also something we absolutely cannot live without.

If we are to know love, we must learn and practise intimacy. Although I was making someone new my reason for existing every week, I had never attempted to trust anyone. I never dreamed of letting them see me act imperfectly, do anything potentially embarrassing or be out of character. I wouldn't let them nurture me or know me; I wanted it to be easier than that. The vulnerability in true intimacy, to be that honest about what you desire and who you are, can feel humiliating. It can be terrifying to be that unscripted, so exposed in the face of possible rejection. You can also realise that as much as you want to be loved, you don't actually know how to receive it.

My old belief wasn't just that love hurts, it was that love destroys – I had to be crucified for it. Spiralling with someone, unable to live without each other while being responsible for each other's downfall, felt very romantic to me. Addicts mistake intensity for intimacy, so it made sense that I was rushing, forcing and chasing what I thought was love, rather than the building of something that required me to be vulnerable. I was in a relationship with the fantasy of what it would be like to be loved, because the thought of experiencing love scared me, as it does for many people who grow up feeling unworthy.

But under the fear I knew I had a big heart. It was something I could never deny or obliterate, and I wanted it back.

A girl who wanted to be loved and to love someone

I had spent a long time lamenting the fact that no one wanted to share my incredible amount of love, when really I'd been haemorrhaging it in the wrong places, with the wrong motives.

By the virtue of our existence, we are worthy of love, but to gain skill with love I needed to practise the act of loving – with no expectation, agenda or notion that convincing someone to love me will be the thing that fixes me.

In her book *All Above Love* (1999), bell hooks describes:

> How different things might be if, rather than saying 'I think I'm in love,' we were saying 'I've connected with someone in a way that makes me think I'm on the way to knowing love.' Or if instead of saying 'I am in love' we say 'I am loving' or 'I will love.'

Rather than love being an object we acquire or achieve, hooks suggests that 'love is as love does' – it is an action. She outlines that love is a transformative force that can lead to radical change, where we can all live fully and freely. Living with a 'love ethic' is to implement this in all areas of our lives.

> We do this by choosing to work with individuals we admire and respect; by committing to giving our all to our relationships; by embracing a global vision wherein we see our lives and our fate as intimately connected to those of everyone on the planet.

I knew what a work ethic was: it's what you get when you don't have generational wealth; it was the only reason I could balance being a full-time alcoholic with being in full-time employment and education for as long as I did. It's not a bad thing when it isn't coming from a place of fear. The act of doing something difficult when you don't always want to is an important skill, especially when you're part of a team. A love ethic is just as important and necessary, to open us to all love is, and all of the many things that exist within it. It is not simply a word allocated as a possibility for only certain relationships, it's a commitment to caring compassionately for someone, acting with loyalty, developing trust, having mercy and empathy, treating each other with respect and creating a sense of safety in our bonds where we and those around us can be ourselves.

A love ethic is not sentimental, it is vital. My family needed my love, after neglecting our relationship. Moving to the USA put a physical distance between us, and I had added emotional distance because I was scared that an alcoholic maniac wasn't the daughter they wanted. My friends needed my love, as a priority and not just something secondary to a partner. The women in my twelve-step meetings needed my love, as an active participant in helping one another. My work needed my love, as an act of service and not something to endure or obsess over. Sad strangers on the Tube needed my love; my neighbours needed my love; the cashier who was being screamed at by the customer before me needed my love; the artists, musicians and writers I enjoyed needed my love; the people who I would normally ignore needed my love; the environment needed my love; people fighting for a better world need my love. I thought, as an experiment, *What if I did everything from a place of love and don't just focus on the areas that get me laid?* In my choices I asked myself, 'Is this loving?'

I've sometimes thought it's easier not to love, because then I lose nothing. But now I argue that we lose nothing by loving. If I feel my love is wasted, then I had an agenda or was looking for a fix. When I love from the core of that tender-hearted girl who just wanted to share that feeling, I am in line with and operating from my true values.

When love is an action for no other reason than adding my love to the world, I'm less likely to be manipulative or to make decisions out of fear. Love isn't there to be sucked out of something or someone, it is something to generate. Like anything, if you feed it, it grows. This requires us not only to love, but to allow ourselves to be loved as the necessary other half of the giving and receiving of love. Being sober means we are capable of being present, generous and loyal. Everyone has the type of love that can transform a person, when put in the right places.

While there is an addictive streak in my patterns and behaviours, I reject the idea that love is simply a transactional function of evolution, that we are just trading interactions to feel good or to avoid the risk of being alone. Even if that is true, it runs alongside the ineffable and transformative connectivity of meeting someone who feels like home. I choose to see the synchronicities, and revel in the improbabilities of the significant relationships in my life. It's too easy to get cynical about love in a cynical world, but I am as bored of cynicism as I was by my old patterns of destructive behaviour – which were rooted not only in pain, but in a great cynicism that everything was material and I would find meaning if I just consumed enough of it.

I am a romantic for the entire planet, for the view of the sun rising above the abandoned gas cylinders out of my window, for the smell of wisteria on the walk to my best friend's house, for the moments when I see someone look down at their phone and smile, for my friends in their studios working on their books, exhibitions and music right now, for the way the ocean lends a pulse to the world without my effort, and for the group of elderly people I see walking around Victoria Park together, still taking care of each other in the ways they can after all these years.

And as I was addressing and reforming my relationship with love, I also hoped that one day I would have a romantic relationship with a partner, with the elaborate memories about the time we bought a plant pot on a Tuesday afternoon and the nonsense words that only we understand. Someone I could grow with, loving each day with our actions.

And now about sex

When I was 16, a man I was sleeping with told me I was bad at sex. I didn't know you could be bad at sex. I thought sex was just men doing stuff to you.

From that point on, like many people who had sex thrown upon them before they could choose it, I abdicated into a highly sexualised character, one who couldn't be hurt because I wanted to make it seem like it was my choice. Sex became an outward display that I was a libertine. I wanted to bewitch people through my dark art, to seem like the ultimate pleasure seeker who desired nothing more than to chase the prey and get the kill, loving every second of it. I wanted them to think this, so I would think this. I wanted to dilute the harm of the past, pack it into nothingness. I would always want sex, so no one could harm me by taking it when I didn't.

I felt like sex was the most accessible entry point for love. In many ways it wasn't about the sex at all. I just wanted to be held, treasured, made to feel like the only thing someone cared about, even if it was just because someone was in my mouth. It was the same satisfaction I felt performing on-stage – which left me so hungry in the dressing room, because deep down I knew they didn't care about me like I wanted them to, they were just enjoying the performance. Having sex with people who didn't care about my dignity, pleasure or safety was cutting without the knife, and it didn't leave a scar.

For a long time the idea of being sexy, sensual or confident was only comfortable when I was drunk. I needed to drink so I didn't remember how it felt to have the hands of my abuser on my body or think about the fact that more than one person has said that my body 'doesn't bother them', as if sleeping with a woman with belly fat is a noble act of self-sacrifice. Sober sex felt like sex for people who weren't as fucked up and damaged, or the delusionally confident. Sex required a necessary level of dissociation. I'd learned my lines, I could hit my marks and I could forget myself in the show. I would lose myself in the performance to protect the girl who was frozen in a pocket of pain. I escaped being a full and nuanced human by reducing myself to this one quality that I didn't even enjoy, which felt like the only thing of value I brought to relationships.

I drank so I didn't have to process it. I got sober and it all came back.

In sobriety, I wanted to affirm to myself that I was having sex, not having sex done to me. I wanted to challenge the idea that I needed it to happen immediately, for fear of being lonely or losing the chance, and remember that among all of my escapades there were very genuine people who wanted to treat me well, and I just wasn't in a place to receive it because it would mean addressing all the things I wasn't ready to face. I wanted to remind myself that sex was supposed to be fun, and it was something I could and wanted to do sober.

A woman who I shared an almost identical abuse story with once told me: 'Don't be a victim. Have good sex.' Her directness shocked me, but as I listened to her, I recognised that I had been a victim, because I was the victim of sexual crime. Then I had calcified there, feeling there was no way out and no other possible future. I was now seeing that it was possible to change my ideas and beliefs about myself as a sexual person, and I had the opportunity to act upon it – as a survivor, I wanted to have good sex.

The first time I had sober sex, we were drinking tea at my flat after a dinner date, and I was still arrested with embarrassment over pronouncing the 'bass' in 'sea bass' like the 'bass' in 'double bass'. I couldn't let it go. Whenever there was a pause in the conversational flow I brought it back up, saying I was a musician, I'd only seen the word written down, and that we could never go back there because the waiter knows I'm a bog-dweller who has never been to a nice restaurant before. He kept telling me it was fine, he didn't think any less of me and I could drop it. By the time I refilled our mugs we were laughing about it, and about all the strange hang-ups that we have over being perceived by a person we want to like us. On our previous date I told him I wasn't ready to have sex yet, and braced myself for mockery or coercion. When neither came, I felt an unusual safety, which made me want to have sex with him. I was pretty sure it would happen tonight. I remembered that he knew my favourite flowers were tulips, and no one had ever known that about me. I wondered if this was what people who could have just a glass of wine with dinner thought about before sex. My next realisation was that I could feel his hands, and it made me think of spiders. First tulips, now spiders. Maybe I just wasn't supposed to have sex.

I remembered that someone had suggested using my senses as an anchor, so I chose touch. I breathed, and focused on where my hands were, on him, only him, someone I had built trust with, who had made it clear he was willing to receive my no. His hands sunk into me, and it wasn't such a bad feeling any more. I moved through where my senses met him – how I could hear our skin touching, taste desire and smell that peppery smell of his aftershave. I felt tingly – not the tingly that was a precursor to a dissociative episode where I find myself half an hour later sitting at a train station wondering how I got there, but a good tingly. But a high-speed train of an old fear threw itself through my brain. What if I wasn't actually good at sex? He asked me what I wanted, and I worried that I couldn't do the splits sober. But his question was an invitation he wanted to honour, so I asked him to go slowly. I could not believe that what I wanted was so boring, but when I asked myself what I wanted, that's what my body answered. It was a small voice that knew I wanted this to start slow. We could work out the rest as we went.

Moving on from a life of being a bit fucked up around sex and love

If you've had an emotional rock bottom around sex where the scream inside says, 'Enough' there is an opportunity to change the focus to nourishing every area of your relationship with yourself, including your relationship to your sensuality. You can explore masturbation not just as a quick fix for stress or an opportunity to procrastinate. You can invite your imagination and make observations around what you enjoy and how you feel as a sexual being outside of anyone's expectations. You can go at the pace where you can breathe into it and ride that breath with waves of excitement, feeling parts of your body that have a tendency to shut down. Involuntary sensations aren't just trauma responses. While there are waves of intensity, you don't have to respond to them with fear – they aren't always invasive intrusions.

Learning more about my own touch made me curious about how it would feel to be touched by someone else again, in a frame of mind where I was enjoying my desire and not feeling consumed by a need for something sex couldn't give me. It was easy to consider, but a much more difficult thing to explore.

Katherine Angel in *Tomorrow Sex Will be Good Again*, (2021) explains:

> Sex is an interaction, resolutely social and interpersonal – far closer to other social phenomena than it is unlike them. Sex, like anything social, is a process, a development, an unfolding. Sex is a conversation, and like any conversation, can be promising, and can yield on that promise – or it can disappoint.

Like any conversation, whether it is committed, casual or a mixture of the two, it is more interesting when we are honest with our motivations, and communicate them honestly with the people involved, to reduce the chance of putting ourselves or anyone else in a position to be hurt. It is safe when I consider who I am engaging with and remain aware, conscious and willing to do the uncomfortable thing of expressing myself truthfully. It is curious when I follow where it goes, allowing for flexibility, but am unwilling to betray myself. If we are contorting ourselves to sustain a sexual relationship, it might not be one that serves us. It has the meaning we give it, and staying honest makes it a place to explore.

When examining our relationship with sex we don't have to vilify it, just address our patterns. Throughout sobriety we get a new relationship to our body and senses, and we begin to hold ourselves in higher regard and treat ourselves differently as a result of that. This puts us in a position to explore deeply the sensations of our body from a place of safety.

When you are honestly working out your relationship to sex, it can sometimes feel like you are either permanently horny or dead inside. Rather than feeling broken, you can acknowledge that your libido is movable and desires can change. There is no permanent state; it is another thing to find the rhythm of.

Ignoring your needs is not loving, and it can turn sex into a bargaining chip or a future resentment. Saying what you need builds sexual integrity, which isn't purity-based ideas from archaic roles, it's simply acting in line with what feels good for you and seeing if the person you are naked with is a good match for that. As much as we are allowed to ask for clarity, we must be receptive to other people's need for the same. It might be awkward, but awkwardness will not kill us – it's a bridge. What's more, everyone else is as awkward and insecure as we are. There is no normal, and no universal standard of 'good', only a decided pace and comfort level that is mutually agreed upon, and done with enthusiasm. You don't have to have the best sex of your life every time with every person, and you won't be sexually compatible with everyone. Not all partners are able to meet your needs, and we all have to learn how each other works.

Changing patterns doesn't just mean changing behaviours, it changes your beliefs about yourself. It's not just changing how you feel, it's changing how you think. I eventually stopped feeling like a broken toy. I wanted to be wanted, but it was different – I wanted someone to want me, to share it in something we both enjoyed. Sex became one of the many ways I show love, as well as playfulness, silliness and pleasure. I wanted not only to have done it, but the tastes, sounds, scents and touch of every moment of it. I wanted to throw my head back and see galaxies, and give myself over to someone's savage care. It took practice to get to that place, but it's not long division or Chopin's

Études – it's gradually learning how to enjoy everything a body has to offer.

Love is infinite, energy is finite. Use it wisely, in the right direction

Nicholas and I spend a lot of time talking about love. He told me one day, during one of these sprawling conversations, that one of the things he loves the most about me is that my pursuit of love took me to some desolate places, but I was always willing to bounce back and try again. It takes a lot to love as hopefully as this, and if we can still love, be ready to love again after what we have lost, then we are the strongest of all of them.

We do not need to be perfectly healed to be loved. We are never at a place in our healing journey where we are 'ready', and from that point we will never have any troubles with love. We might have issues, hang-ups and fears, and they cannot be worked out in our head – they are worked out when we get in the ring with what we're struggling with, and face it.

XI. Dating

Sometimes I believe that love is as natural as the tides, and sometimes I believe that love is an act of will. Sometimes I believe that some people are better at love than others, and sometimes I believe that everyone is faking it. Sometimes I believe that love is essential, and sometimes I believe that the only reason love is essential is that otherwise you spend all of your time looking for it.
— Norah Ephron, *Heartburn* (1983)

When you wish your body knew that fight or flight was for life-and-death situations, not sober dating. When you want to be known and loved, but that level of vulnerability feels like it needs at least three mind-altering chemicals. When your dating patterns are a little bit feral, and you want to do it differently this time.

I had started talking to a guy I really hit it off with. We laughed at the prompts on Hinge, and the standard responses – how everyone wants you not to take yourself too seriously and to be spontaneous, when we both liked planning things, and agreed that it's kind of OK to take yourself at least a little bit seriously. We still laugh about it now, over dinners and walks in the park. At least I think we would; he ghosted me because I wouldn't let him put a belt around my neck on the second date, and I had to go back to the drawing board again.

I ended things with Liam for good just after I turned three years sober in March 2021, not that there was much to end – I simply stopped replying and he made no attempt to lure me back, confirming what people kept trying to tell me: that he did not care whether I lived or died. I then took a break from dating, to develop an even more nurturing relationship with myself, treating myself with the care and commitment I always thought could only be given by a romantic partner. I took myself on dates to museums and coffee shops, watched the films that I said I wanted to but felt I didn't have time for and bought myself flowers once a week. I was celibate, and felt sexier than I ever had. I dressed how I wanted to and my body started moving differently, with more ease and less performance. I read more books than I had in years. Initially I thought I'd just take a few weeks off the apps. It turned into six months after I discovered how good it felt to treasure my own life consciously, and to have the space to do exactly what I wanted with it for no other reason than it was my precious life, and I could. But eventually I felt ready and willing to start dating again, not because I would be totally untriggered, but because I felt strong enough to be triggered and not have it derail my entire sense of self. I also wanted to see how it would feel to practise intimacy and receive loving treatment in a romantic relationship; to recognise and extract myself from situations with untappable potential, and maybe get some orgasms out of it.

I was in a café in East London, running my Hinge profile past a friend for her approval. After she had verified that I had all the necessary pictures and prompts to indicate I was a fun, very normal, very chill person with hobbies and interests, we swiped through some of the local single people. Scrolling through someone's basic info, I noticed that they had selected that they drank 'sometimes'.

I squinted at the screen for a moment. 'It says he sometimes drinks, what does that mean?' My friend – not an alcoholic – sighed. 'I can't believe I actually have to explain this to you.' And I remembered that there are people out there who don't just drink either all the time or not at all.

In my dating hiatus I realised that I'd never actually really dated before; I was more likely to fall into a pattern with someone who would put up with me, and eventually move in with them and discover who they actually were. I would fall in love, make commitments, then get to know them, rather than the other way around. I would rather be right than happy, and stay certain in an unsatisfying, familiar dynamic, than risk hoping for a new one. I wouldn't consider whether I could grow towards a shared goal with the person; these weren't things I'd even thought to consider when I was swiping. I'd usually be looking for a humanoid cigarette who would talk at me, condescendingly, about Tarkovsky.

I prayed to the universe, asking it to stop sending me piranhas of the mind on dating apps. I received the message 'Stop fucking choosing them' back. This time around I was going to see people as people, not use them as my only source of self-esteem when the going was good, and co-sign my shame and feeling of hopelessness when their thumbs mysteriously broke and I wasn't their muse any more.

When I'd made dating profiles in the past, I'd prided myself on being a girl who could drink. I had stories, I had many cute quips and witticisms about my ability and enthusiasm for drinking. I needed to make it abundantly clear that I could drink anyone under the table, or at least have it as a quirky part of my identity. Most of all, I didn't want to present as anyone close to the person I actually was. I could happily have my drunk-hellion-slut-princess-act be rejected, because she wasn't near to the softer parts of me that I wanted to protect at all costs.

My dating while drinking: a history of misadventure

I once told someone from Tinder that I was Russian, and committed to this lie so hard that if I received a call when we were together, I would answer and start babbling in Russian (with a very limited, opera-based vocabulary), which was very confusing for my mother – who is, in fact, not Russian. I told someone I was married to stop him from getting too close to me – something I'm fairly sure he saw through, because he asked to see my passport and I told him I'd lost it, despite the fact that I'd only just got back from a gig in Italy.

Once I organised a date with a work colleague and thought I'd have a drink to calm my nerves. I ended up sitting in my flat doing vodka shots by myself all night. That wasn't where our romance ended, however; we met on a night out a few years later, and I got banned from a club because of what has since been referred to as 'the Cathouse nipple incident'. The saddest part was that I really liked him, but I couldn't engage with him sober or on a human-to-human level because I was too nervous. After that I started seeing someone who would always yell in the pub that they needed to play 'Brown Eyed Girl'. Sick of it, I told him my eyes were grey, and he replied it wasn't for me, it was for my friend who he would rather be with. After a fight, he moved to Ireland and blocked me, and I harassed his sister on Facebook for money he owed me, from when he got kicked out of his flat and moved in with me after two months of dating.

The first date I went on in America was with a woman who was so beautiful I could barely believe she was even slightly interested in me. That was a discomfort I simply needed to be drunk for, and instead of that making me flirtatious and engaged, it made me shut-down and evasive. I forgot my card on our first date, which was probably less embarrassing than the alternative of trying to pay and having my card declined – because by that point in my drinking my account was absolutely empty.

There were endless first-date experiences when I simply was not in attendance. I was a sad and solitary person nodding my way through the conversation, keeping a watchful eye on their drink to either suggest another round or comment on the fact that they were drinking too slowly. There were the dates when they said they ought to stop drinking to keep a clear head, and I encouraged them to take more, to potentially elicit some drunken praise or keep us in a comfortable state of delusion together. There were the dates when they said I seemed like a lot of fun, and I thought, *Thank God, they think I'm drinking because it's fun, and not because I feel like I need to.*

Doing it differently

After my break from dating, I met Shane, a friend of a friend. I met him at the Tube station near his flat and suggested we walk to find somewhere to go. This was a horrendous idea, because I am incapable of making a decision and he didn't know the area at all. Shane had very sad and sexy eyes, was from the USA and shared my trauma of spending too many years in music school. He had been here for a year setting up his company's London office, and still only operated from his American phone. I had done the exact same thing when I moved to America; it was a perfect way not to commit to anything – not even the country you are legally residing in. We had the exact same taste in literature, and when I got nervous and started talking about ghosts, he ran with it, and we excitedly discussed how haunted Colorado was.

He happily bought me tonic waters, satisfied with the fact that I was turning out to be a very cheap date. After I told him my experience of seeing a ghost, a frontier-era spectre in the corner of my room during my studio artist contract in Colorado, he abruptly asked me if I was in recovery. This was a hard left turn, but given how comfortable I was with him, I told him that I was three years sober. He started to talk about his brother, who was currently in rehab for the fifth time.

'It's good you stuck with sobriety. I'm scared he'll stop trying.'

Shane texted me a week later to say he couldn't keep seeing me, because he had got another girl pregnant and needed to support her through the next steps.

It wasn't a perfect start to the world of sober dating, but I had faced embarrassment, disclosure and rejection, and, by some miracle, I did not die.

A doctor from Manchester successfully recognised that I was a non-drinker from my profile, and asked if I was comfortable in bars. I assured him yes, but he suggested we go bowling instead. There was something retro and wholesome about the suggestion, so I agreed. When he showed up and was even more attractive in person, I got nervous and dropped my AirPods. One slip of the finger and I was standing in the middle of the street with 'Hot Stuff' by Donna Summer blasting out of my phone. That wasn't nearly as embarrassing as how awful I am at bowling, but it was a great time doing something I wouldn't have done before. I also wouldn't have gone on five-hour walks around London, a bike tour, a day trip to Berlin (long story) or a bachata class.

The bowling doctor didn't ask me why I didn't drink, but it did come up and was quickly lost in the conversation we were having about our interests and how we walked extremely different paths in life, but had the same niche sense of humour.

Someone asked me if I wanted to go to a particular bar on a first date. I said that I would love to, I just wouldn't be drinking. He politely said he wasn't interested any more, because drinking with his partner was part of his future vision for himself. While this stung, as he had almost paid off his mortgage and had really nice, veiny arms, it was simply a case of incompatibility. No number of green flags, sexy properties and big, veiny arms were going to displace the fact that I couldn't drink without consequences. I didn't mind other people drinking, but I wanted to date people who appreciated the fact that my sobriety is something that is required for me to have safe relationships. It was quite sad to imagine that he couldn't see past the fact that I didn't drink, after finding chemistry in our conversations and agreeing on many important qualifiers, but then again, I probably wouldn't be able to see past the fact that someone enjoyed camping or wanted to go on runs with me (two horrors beyond my comprehension).

After going on a few dates with a writer and comedian with a really sweet cat, I did the texting rounds, telling everyone how excited I was that I'd met someone I really liked. Shortly after, he said he wasn't feeling a connection and wanted to be friends. I was honest and said that I wasn't in the market for friends I felt a sexual attraction to; I was looking for someone to date. I called my friend and furiously ranted that I couldn't believe he didn't want me – I was a young woman with strong sobriety, great friends, an upwardly mobile career (debatable) and some degree of emotional intelligence. She told me that I didn't need him to validate those things for them to be true. She was right, but I still bemoaned the fact that it seemed so unfair because he was perfect for me. She laughed and replied that if he was perfect for me, then he'd want to date me.

Sober dating was working, I was getting more practice – and it was becoming fun. A lot of the dates were one-hit wonders; some of them softly fell off when the conversation died from one end, some of them had a more deliberate end when we discovered that we wanted different things. I had spent so much of my life praying that the next relationship would be the one, but dating from a position of actually liking myself created a new belief that there might not actually be 'the one' and I'd still be OK. When you start to like yourself as a sober single person, regardless of what the other person thinks of you, things feel less jagged and urgent. It makes 'single' not a state of being that you are simply tolerating until someone comes along to free you from it. It means that you can be truly open to a connection that is more than simply settling with the first person who shows you some affection out of a fear that you've found the only person who will accept you.

Love and dating are connected to our most fundamental attachment needs, which in our infancy were necessary for survival, so it makes perfect psychological sense that love, and the prospect of abandonment, rejection and the disappointment that lies therein, inevitably presents a risk of losing our fucking minds. It can make the stakes seem extremely high, which we must match by being a perfect person, and have them believe it and relay it back to us, because someone's approval seems just so much more valuable than our own.

I was describing this to my friend Christian, and he simply replied: 'Dating should be fun and easy. Never audition; you are the prize.'

But what do I DO?

When organising a date, it is the standard procedure that people will normally ask you to go for a drink. If you feel bored and annoyed by drunk people or the bar scene, there really is no reason why you have to make that your only option, despite it being the most obvious one. We don't get sober to be uncomfortable, bored or irritated unnecessarily – there's enough discomfort, boredom and irritation in other areas of life as it is. However, if you are confident in your sobriety and comfortable around alcohol, then you can be sure of going and being a sober person there. It is always useful to consider whether you are going to a pub or a bar as a neutral social space to meet someone, or to pick up a second-hand thrill and give yourself an excuse to fuck around and find out if you can drink 'like a normal person' again.

If you are going to a bar or pub, you can look ahead to see whether or not they have non-alcoholic options that interest you. If they have a dedicated non-alcoholic section with a variety of drinks on offer, then it is an indicator that there is a demand for that at that venue, and it is more likely to have a vibe you will be more comfortable with as a non-drinker. If they have food, even better, because busying myself with a charcuterie board on a date has been an unexpected pleasure of sober dating. It is probably not the best idea to go somewhere that has romanticised attachments to it, or somewhere you've been dragged out of at 2 a.m. because you were scream-crying over the phone at your ex in the toilets.

In my life as an active alcoholic, the thought of a daytime date was for losers and geriatrics. That was until I discovered the beautiful simplicity of a coffee date – how it was perfectly inexpensive (unless you live in London) and you could leave at any time. The idea of feeling trapped on a date, especially sober, is what puts most people off dinner dates, as it's a large amount of time (and money) to commit to with a person you aren't sure you like yet. There is also an imposed structure to dining out that can be off-putting. That said, a dinner date doesn't have to be a sit-down affair with three courses; it can be as formal or as informal as you like. One of my friends is a staunch anti-dinner-date advocate. I asked her what she did for dates and she simply replied: 'Lunch.' There are more options than you think, even if it's just selecting another meal. I, for one, am a die-hard dinner fan, because I enjoy sitting down, eating food and being admired in foxy lighting.

One of the most fun aspects of sober dating is the freedom to be creative outside of just 'going for a drink'. Going to galleries is a fun way to engage with someone's creativity or sense of the world around them, museums let me see what lights them up and gives us a lot to talk about. Engaging with local theatre and shows not only makes me realise how much is happening in my area, but helps me to find new things I'm interested in and want to do more of. The cinema is a risk, because it can lead to some awkward parallel sitting and not knowing what to do with your hands, but afterwards it can be an opportunity for me to practise saying whether I liked something or not, and not be obsessed with trying to say the right or smart thing.

In your experience of dating yourself and connecting with your interests, you will have more of an idea of what you want to do for fun, and suggesting creative ideas is a great first-date move, as most of us are quite bored with the same routine. Another bonus is that, even if the date is terrible, you've at least done something unexpected with your day and have a good story.

How do I tell someone I'm sober?

Having 'sober' on a dating profile may seem like a risk, like you're saying too much. In early sobriety I thought the only thing I had going for me was the fact that I didn't drink – it was honestly one of the only things I wanted to talk about. Someone would ask me how I was and I would reply, 'Seventy-eight days sober, thank you very much.' But when I started dating again, I was less sure of being transparent about my sobriety, with people who didn't know me or have the intimate knowledge of recovery that I did.

It made me realise that in some areas, I was still holding

onto the belief that my sobriety was something that made me separate from 'normal' people. It was easy to feel accepted with people who knew what it's like to piss the bed on a one-night stand or had a similar sense of freedom in choosing not to drink, but dating is one of the ultimate challenges of taking your acceptance of yourself into the wild. When I told my friend about this she laughed and said, 'You're just meeting someone you don't know for the first time – who's to say they're "normal"?' She paused, and added, 'Please don't tell them on the first date that you used to piss the bed after one-night stands.'

There are lots of ways to say you don't drink. You can say, 'It doesn't mix well with me,' 'I enjoy my life and being present for all of it,' or simply, 'I just don't.' I quite like, 'I went pro too young and had a career-ending injury.' You can self-identify as sober and lead with that; there isn't anything abnormal about sobriety, and you can answer any questions in as much or as little detail as you like. If you aren't there yet, you can go into more detail when you feel ready, but until that moment, all they need to know is that you are not drinking. People who acknowledge it can be very respectful, but for some people it barely registers on their radar.

There may be people who are bewildered by it, or maybe even put off. They have the chance to recognise that someone who has questioned their relationship with alcohol and made a decision in the best interests of themselves and those around them is an absolute catch, or let their own perceptions and relationship to alcohol disallow them from doing that. You lose nothing. It's actually easier if they move on, because someone who doesn't appreciate the things you do to ensure your safety and sanity isn't the best match for a sober person.

I have been surprised at how kind and accepting people can

be, and that disclosure is rarely the big event I think it will be. Sometimes sobriety can bring up big feelings in others, like Shane, as there are very few people whose lives haven't been touched in some way by addiction.

When we gain awareness of what we want, we become more adept at recognising what we don't want

I went on a date with an artist I thought was absolutely too cool for me. He immediately asked me if I was in recovery, if I worked the twelve steps and if I had any stories for him. He then angled to spend the whole date sharing the worst things that had ever happened to us, a fast-track to imitating emotional intimacy by oversharing before establishing trust. He talked about how he was fascinated by addicts, that I lived with a killer illness and he would keep me safe, drunkenly telling me that he would buy me Maria Callas's house. He eventually admitted he was in love with his ex, which was honestly a relief, because he wanted to cast me in a role I wasn't willing to play any more.

Then there was a photographer who showed healthy concern that he was over twelve years older than me, but raised genuine alarm at the fact that I didn't drink because, 'How am I going to get you into bed with me?' People having a drink to soothe their nerves may be a perfectly normal thing to do for some people, but if someone sees alcohol as a necessary appeasement into sex, then they have no business being in a sexual relationship with you.

When you have more awareness of the person in front of you, fewer things go unnoticed. I noticed the techniques some people would use to convince me I needed their approval, to make the broken parts of me want them. I had no idea how subtle negging was, I never questioned veiled insults before, I thought I deserved them. On one date, the guy leaned over the table and said it was cute how nervous I was. It was a strange and disarming thing to say, because I wasn't nervous – it was an obvious power play, but it did make me doubt myself for a second. My body felt very strange in his presence. I thought that maybe I was too weird to be loved, and that maybe I needed to be drunk to do this after all. Something new happened when he ran his hand across my tattoo of an orca on my upper thigh and told me it was 'very cute, very Nineties – it's sweet, you think that's cool'. I realised I didn't like this person, I didn't feel good around him, and I didn't have to stay if I didn't want to. It wasn't anything to do with me, I just didn't like him. I said, 'This isn't working for me, best of luck,' and left.

When we are not having a good time or feel uncomfortable, it makes us susceptible to drinking or sacrificing our authenticity for relief. Choosing to be sober is one of the most potent ways not to abandon yourself, and this is the black-belt of practising that. As your intuition returns you start to be able to tell the difference between something being uncomfortable because it is new or difficult, and something being uncomfortable because you are in a situation you don't have to or want to be in. It takes presence, patience and a conscious awareness of our levels of safety and bravery to leave, block or decline. The more you connect with your body with the clarity that sobriety affords, the more you can recognise your own signals rather than doubt them – enabling you to leave potentially unsafe or unsatisfying experiences. Eventually, the people you gravitate towards, who don't push boundaries or have expectations, become more interesting to you, and the pattern changes.

Not everyone is out there doing their best; some people are doing their worst – and I have probably dated most of them. Changing my attitudes and patterns did change the type of people I dated, but my traumatised thinking can warp the idea of 'you attract what you put out' into thinking it was my vibes or energy that was responsible for inviting abuse into my life, and thereby my fault. I can't keep that narrative alive. I can, however, recognise my agency, and while it shouldn't be that I have to take such protective measures – we shouldn't be impervious to abuse to avoid being abused (it should be on others not to abuse us) – I will go bravely into the unknown, because I know some people want what I want, like in any area of human life and society.

Some lessons I've learned during dating like it was my job**

Dating is putting in an effort and surrendering the outcome. Dating means you will face disappointment and rejection; that is simply a fact of dating, whether you're sober or not. To get good at dating, and to gain resilience around those two sensitive issues, you have to go on dates.

Consider your dating patterns in the past that haven't worked for you, and whether you want to let them go. If you have moved

---

** In twelve-step fellowships it is sometimes suggested that you do not date in the first year of sobriety, in order to protect and prioritise your recovery. You can do whatever you like in recovery as long as you can live with the consequences, but dating in early sobriety can be a distraction from facing yourself, and puts you in a vulnerable position during a period where you are already very emotionally vulnerable.

too quickly in the past, work out some measures to have in place so that you can take it slowly. If you have been fearful of rejection to the point of being passive or evasive, play through in your head what it would be like to be brave, say what you want or be direct.

Consider what you want out of the experience. 'Looking for a relationship' and 'looking for some fun' can exist in the same space, as dating should always be fun and being open to possibilities allows that, but if you are constantly going for people who 'aren't looking for anything serious right now' when you are wanting a committed partnership then you are dating your idea of someone and not the reality. Dating someone with the intention of changing their mind is a lot less fun than being patient with someone who doesn't need to be convinced to want what you want.

Trying to get love out of an unavailable person doesn't make you more lovable, but it can kill your self-esteem. Nicholas always says, 'I love love, I would die for love, but love will never ask me to sacrifice my dignity.' I can be confused or uncertain about where a connection is going, but I never want to be confused or uncertain about how someone feels about me. We are allowed to ask, so long as we are prepared for the answer.

I wrote down and committed to (that's the hard part) some areas I will never return to: I will not date married men (even if they are a hot dad) or people who remind me of my ex. I will not date people who have violated my consent or expressed explicitly that they are still in love with their ex. I will not date people who are not capable of consistency or are inconsiderate of my time. I will not be the most easily discarded option – that doesn't do it for me any more. I will not date people who live in different countries or who won't let me get close to them. I do not date liars, abusers, manipulators or confusers. You don't need to change them – you just need not to date them.

From dating myself, I realised who I wanted to be in a relationship: available, faithful and as accepting of their vulnerabilities as they hopefully will be about mine. I also gained some idea of who I wanted to be in a relationship with; I wanted to date people who are active in their friendships, interested in their jobs and ask questions. It helped shift my thinking to realising that it wasn't a luxury to actually like the person you are dating, it's kind of the point.

Watch out for future-tripping (throwing ourselves mentally further down the line based on the little we do know and creating either disastrous or fairytale outcomes), and getting hooked on how someone makes us feel rather than who they are. When meeting people it is easy for us mentally to jump to the finish, where we get the hit or the payoff. This can look like identifying a few qualifying factors and deciding, 'Yes, this is the one,' and boarding the relationship escalator with someone you barely know. It can look like fast-tracking the process in our mind to 'the rest of my life' and writing out a script to deal with the uncertain idea of an unforeseeable future. It can also look like mentally living out every terrible thing that could possibly go wrong in an attempt to grip for control, so when our worst fears are realised we will be OK with it. But if we lower the stakes, and realise we're just getting more information as we go, we can be exactly where we are – getting to know someone gradually and seeing if our values align. Taking it as it comes can exist in the same space as being honest about what we want.

Sometimes I want to just download all of that information

and install it into other people's brains when I meet them, to avoid all of that conversation and getting-to-know-you bullshit. Then I have to remind myself that the conversation and the getting-to-know-you bit is actually the joy of meeting new people. You can't take lasting connection like a pill.

It's never wasted time if you're having fun. Fun is never wasted.

Someone not texting back immediately doesn't mean that they don't prioritise you. They could just be busy, and, as someone they don't know yet, you're in the appropriate position in their list of priorities. It might not be that deep, and not everyone has an agenda. This is important to remember in moments of doubt, but if those moments turn into patterns, it makes more sense to weigh their stated intentions with evidence, so you aren't trying to nurture a bond when you are on the backburner. Time is the most valuable resource and I don't have enough of it to make time for people who won't make time for me.

Conflict can be resolved with communication or separation. If our safety or sanity is threatened, we don't need to continue making good-faith assumptions, but sometimes trusting that someone has good intentions and seeking further clarity can stop us from treating people as disposable when we're scared of uncertainty. This is a time to use your skills. Navigating misunderstandings or conflict so that you both feel seen and heard can show you vital parts of a person and give you necessary information. Advocating for ourselves, hearing another point of view and compromising are only things we can find in discomfort. Other people are allowed to be messy and imperfect, as much as we are allowed to be messy and imperfect – you can find the messy imperfections you can live with together.

Many conflicts can be a conversation first, and it's sometimes, though not always, better in person (sending paragraphs isn't always a useful way to be seen and heard, which as a writer is very frustrating, but not as frustrating as receiving a wall of text from a writer).

There's no dating template that works for everyone, there is no pre-made formula or set rule that simplifies it. Some people swear by meeting immediately, while others like to text for a while; some people identify the feeling of fireworks as them mistaking the activation of fight or flight for chemistry, while others require it to get to a second date. You find your own pattern and your own preferences based on what works for you, and no one else can do it for you.

You're not the only one who is vulnerable here. We're all just a bag of neuroses that wants to love and be loved. You get to be sober and sane in your relationships now, to make something sustainable and manageable. All that being said, I did book a five-day trip to Montenegro with a man I'd met on Instagram, so sobriety hasn't made me sane enough to always make good decisions.

I learned that I needed to stop being so utterly convinced I knew everything, and that I know exactly how things are going to play out. After my first date with the bowling doctor, Chris, I texted my friend, 'I had so much fun, but I'm never going to hear from that man again as long as I live,' and five months later, he was the one I ended up in a relationship with. A year and a half later, five years sober, I moved all of my Himalayan salt lamps into his flat, and I'm writing this on the little blue desk he got me.

PART V

Looking back, with the intention of moving forward – how to live with the past and feel hopeful about the future.

XII. Regret

> *You initiate your own healing by re-integrating lost or fragmented portions of your essential self. In order to accomplish this task, you need a strong desire to become whole again.*
> – Peter Levine, *Walking the Tiger: Healing Trauma* (1997)

When what you left behind is still dragging at you. When you wish none of it had happened and you could take it all back. When you can have compassion for everyone, except your own stupid self.

I used to think the greatest chance I'd ever been given was the chance to study music at Yale, and even then I drafted emails trying to withdraw because it felt like a chance that was too good to be mine. During my move to New Haven I held the sides of the aeroplane sink, hungover and begging myself to get it together – promising myself it would be different this time. This promise didn't last until the airport bar, where I got drunk on red wine (I didn't normally drink wine, so it didn't count) and spent two hours aggressively flirting with the waiter, because I thought having a boyfriend who worked at an airport would be convenient. I didn't think I'd be sober six months later.

Even though I started my sobriety before I had lost everything, even though I was young and might have had one round left in me, choosing sobriety was my last stop. It wasn't the story I'd imagined for myself, but it was the entrance to a more interesting one.

Sometimes I love thinking about my old life, because at one point drinking really worked for me, and it was fun. Living on the edge, convincing yourself you have nothing to lose, can be exhilarating — when you're grabbing at your life by the fingertips there's always enough adrenalin to propel you into the next storyline. Nothing inside me wants to go back there, but sometimes I miss it. Missing something but not wanting it back is one of those unusual conflicts where two things exist in complete opposition; somehow both are true in their own way. The past can be easy to romanticise, and though it drove me to a place where I didn't value a single aspect of my existence, it at least felt like it was on my terms. Now I have to show up, feel it all, do all the things I need to do, go to bed and do it again tomorrow. It's not a narrative arc, it's just the daily beauty and complications of being human.

Having to start over made me feel like I was a failure-to-launch case, a bulb that was planted but wouldn't survive the winter. I am starting to see my friends achieve their professional goals, get on the property ladder and start families. I've only just decided I might want to live long enough to start a pension, and I will probably never learn how to parallel park (I am at peace with this). During my 2020 break-up, I thought my chance at love must have passed me by in blackout, and that I'd blown my only chance at it in sobriety. All the explosive, drunken break-ups, screaming matches and sad 'well, we tried' conversations with past partners can get on top of me.

I can fixate on all the money I pissed up the wall during years of active alcoholism. Not just the money I spent on the drink and drugs, but all the money I spent on trying to be a different person, and all the therapy when I lied about my drinking. I think of house deposits and holidays I might have had, and get lost in envy and future-tripping of what I think I will never have. I get stuck in the idea that some people don't have this darkness inside them. I grit my teeth at the idea of how much work I have to do just to *exist*.

I think of all the days of singing practice I wasted being hungover. I think of all the auditions and competitions I didn't show up to or completely bombed in – only to then say, 'Well, I didn't want it anyway!' In 2017 I had a chance to audition for Christine in *Phantom of the Opera* on Broadway after being scouted at a competition. I flew out to New York, prepared the songs they wanted me to sing and then fear made me get drunk in a barbecue restaurant near Times Square rather than go to the callback, choosing the more certain option of 'if I drink this, I will get drunk' rather than 'what if I show up for this, and they think I'm not good enough?' I think of the neglected ambitions I may or may not have had, which passed me by.

I miss people that I have alienated. I wish I'd spent more time with my grandmothers. I really wish I'd nailed that 2017 audition in Philadelphia. I wonder what would have happened if I didn't move around so much, trying to escape who I was.

We can ruminate as pain management. Like any drug, it can be a chosen pain to displace a current discomfort. It gives us a satisfying sense of control, agonising over our choices, finding something to blame. We imagine everything that could have been different, taking us out of reality, as we convince ourselves it's giving us a sharper view of it by thinking about it really hard. It sticks us in an alternate universe to roll miserably about in. We remain in the pain by agonising over what we could have done to avoid it. Fixating on regret, as opposed to processing it, arrests us from getting into reality – a reality that might be better than what we could ever imagine if we engaged with it, with the lessons learned from bitter, sometimes hilarious, unfortunate experience. Getting lost in regret can stop us from thinking about the opportunities we have in front of us that we can completely give ourselves to, and the practical steps we can take to make the necessary changes. It stops us from asking for help or guidance, because we are more preoccupied thinking that we would be fine if we just did something differently in the past.

I have to acknowledge and accept where I am, and the reality outside of my multiverse theory. There was never any other path. I had the experience I had; if I can accept that fully, I can do something with it. It's experience – maybe not the one that I wanted, but it is mine. Accepting my path doesn't mean I have to approve of any of the pain, but I am absolutely prepared to take responsibility for it and choose how I alchemise that pain now. I choose all the mourning, all the grief, all the work it takes to make myself strong enough to carry that, and take a chance at living beyond being defined by the worst things that ever happened to me. If I bypass the grief of my old life by just going back to it, I know that I will either end up in a way worse place or at the beginning of this journey again with more scars. The latter would realistically be the best-case scenario, so I might as well keep going today, seeing as I'm already here.

I have been given chance after chance after chance, and they've never quite gone the way I wanted, or I just threw them away. The biggest chance I've ever been given was getting sober. The days I recognise that I took the greatest chance I ever could take and am living in it today are usually very good days. It was a strange road to get here, but, again, there was no other path.

In defence of the road less travelled

When I was in active addiction there was no achievement or accolade in the world that would have satisfied me, or any amount of emotional or financial security that would have felt like enough. That's the nature of addiction – you get what you want, and immediately need more. There is a limitless supply of the 'next thing' to strive towards.

When I performed the title role in the Daniel Catán opera *Florencia en el Amazonas* I thought I'd finally made it. I was in a custom-made dress, ready to sing an eight-minute aria that felt like it was written for me, for the biggest audience I had ever performed for. The sustained orchestra tremolo was poised underneath me, ready for me to join with the melody, the spotlight drew every eye in the house towards me. As I began, I waited for my anticipated feeling of wholeness, the heady rush of success and the ceasing of my wanting. Instead I heard, from the dark of my shadow thrown behind me, *Fuck, it didn't work.* I was living what I thought my dream was, and still felt the same hollow ache, and the realisation that it was never about any achievement. This was yet another futile quest for the missing piece, the thing that would show them all that I wasn't as fucked up as I felt I was. It's an unusual sensation to feel your entire heart shatter at the exact moment you got exactly what you thought you wanted.

In retrospect, it taught me a lot of what I needed to know. There is no one missing piece that renders you whole. Wholeness takes the time it takes; it is found in many places, and moves backwards and forwards to the rhythm of how we approach life as it happens, along the stages of our growth.

Still, in sobriety I kept thinking that the journey would be all the easier if I just had what I wanted. I had so many wants – to be further along with the landmarks of the adult life I thought I should be living. I know now that if I'd got everything I wanted when I wanted it, I wouldn't have been ready, I wouldn't have been able to keep up. I needed a foundation, one I have now. Whatever I do or do not achieve, living with authenticity I am granted acceptance of myself, which is a much better place to build from. It's also what I wanted the first drink to give me every single time.

When I want to destroy my own peace I have my list of 'Things I believe make me a failure'. It's in these moments that I must remember that the power of sobriety is being able to see things differently. The most powerful thing I can ever believe is: 'I have a choice today.' I can be willing to challenge the stories I'm telling myself, challenge the expectations I have absorbed, and choose a different perspective that is still rooted in reality but doesn't have fear, shame or danger attached to it.

I am childless, and targeted ads for egg freezing and fertility treatments are very quick to remind me that the clock is ticking.

Somewhere in my sobriety I felt comfortable enough to really admit that I wasn't sure if I wanted to be a mother or not. I started genuinely to wonder if it was something I just expected of myself, or something I actually thought I'd want or be good at. Some people try to make me feel better about what they think I lack with a well-meaning, 'Oh, that's OK, you still have time.' but what's more reassuring to me is that I get to remain open to either possibility, that it might or might not happen for me. Either path would have pros and cons; hopefully, I'll be in a position to decide which ones I want to live with.

I do not own property. I have rented over ten places in ten years, and have nothing to show for it apart from constantly ordering parcels to past addresses, a mistrust of landlords and the fact that my bank has no idea where I live. But in that time I have lived in three countries, loving and disliking parts of every single one in a different way. I've been able to go to different places with no ties, and for every frustration I have for not having a security others do, I can reflect on how necessary my moving about was, as I worked things out and had that flexibility to do so. I don't know if I'm ready to settle in one place when there's so many other places for me to fall in love with. As tenant farmers, my parents have spent their whole lives in properties they do not own, and it doesn't stop them from making them theirs. It doesn't take away from my anger at the injustice of the housing market and fears for the future for not just myself but everyone else in my position, but it helps me live with it, and therefore put in the action to change the things I can. I don't actually know if I want to be responsible for a roof or a boiler just yet – I've only just managed to keep my monstera plant alive.

When I broke up with the person I thought I was going

to marry, I felt like I'd squandered my youth, wasted another love story and the body of my twenties. But if that didn't end, I wouldn't have sat on a pier in Penang with Chris, just before my six-year sobriety anniversary, talking about how grateful we were to have met each other as two works in progress, and now we're working some of it out together. We realised we had been in the same bar on Thanksgiving 2017 – he was visiting a friend in New Haven, and I was a non-American with nowhere to go. I am so glad we did not meet then, and did not start our relationship sooner, because we both had a lot to go through before we could begin.

I spent decades of my life thinking I wanted to work as a classical musician, and now my musicianship is largely used for singing 'Happy Birthday' (bringing a gun to a knife fight, because I do not sing, I perform) and teaching people who have the same dreams I no longer align with. This sometimes feels like an enormous loss, like the sacrifices and commitment of my training were for nothing, because there is no concrete evidence of what it amounted to. But the decision to step back from my career in that field came when I gave myself the choice to try something different and see if that felt good for me, rather than keep doing it because I felt like I was supposed to. I realised, when stepping back felt like a relief, that I'm allowed to change my mind. Changing course is as valid a part of a journey as staying on the track, and sometimes it's the necessary course of action. I thought that my 'recovery story' would be that I overcame the odds and became a famous opera singer. It felt like the necessary happy ending to give my trauma meaning, and to make all of the work worth it. I started considering that my 'recovery story' could simply be one where I enjoyed the life I was living now, and that could be more meaningful and satisfying than any happy ending I could imagine.

It's a scary realisation to acknowledge that you can change your mind, and not the news people want to hear when you're home for Christmas and they ask, 'How is the singing going?' But it is also the most exciting thing I have going for me. I chose my first career path when I was a teenager who couldn't even see herself living very long. I can give myself a little bit of flexibility now to see what is out there, rather than freak out that my plan didn't turn out the way I thought it would. In the time I spent training in this rigorous field, I learned all the things I needed and wanted to learn, which moulded me, and eventually brought me to a rock bottom that almost killed me, but brought me right here, right on time. I can be so many things outside of 'singing girl', which is how people I haven't seen in a few years still refer to me (among other, perhaps less flattering things). I can be strong enough to let go of other people's expectations of me. No one thought I'd ever be sober, so maybe I'll always be keeping them guessing.

I'm glad my journey has been unexpected. I have been given the ability to forgive and be forgiven, jobs that challenged and eventually thrilled me, immigration dramas that seemed like disasters but landed me where I needed to be, responsibilities I resented that eventually made me a safe adult, and peace of mind after straightening up everything I had made crooked. I did not want any of these things, but I am glad they were what I was given. Growth can happen when you focus less on an old idea of what you should be doing, or should have done, and put all of your attention solely on what you are doing – right in this intersection of space and time, fiercely and fully present in the moment you are in. There, you can imagine a life without the barometer of a perceived self, and get more acquainted with the present one.

Some people walk through their life without reaching the depths and heights we did, and having that as part of our story is an asset. The places our darkness has taken us to has shaped us in a way that we can never fully separate from – and why would we? It has made us who we are. It's where we found out things we couldn't have found any other way.

Our recovery is not just about or for us. We know the way out of hell, we've done it, and we let other people know it's possible by the nature of our existence. There is no worthier story to have – one where you shipwrecked your life, found yourself in the debris and, rather than drown, you fought for your life, and found something to create a new journey with. In the process of that, the worst things that ever happened to you become part of a bigger story. Carrying that, even laughing about it, can inspire someone else by the simple reality that you are someone who survived. You survived something that people presently in that place don't believe they will. Not only did you make it out of hell, you know the way, and can make the path clearer for other people, and maybe even hold the guiding light.

We need to grow because we have so much inside us – the pain of our past is just one side of it. We deal with first things first, the rest follows, and a few years later we think, *Fuck, I really have come a long way*. The exact place we need to be might very well be right here. The grieving process is not linear when we're learning to let go of resentment and regret to make space for gratitude, but on the best of days, I can say I don't regret taking the long way around. It's been a hell of a ride.

Even though I felt like a bulb that wouldn't make it through the winter, maybe I was just taking time because I was planted deep, finding the right place to stick my roots. I don't know if that's how it works, I'm not a gardener (still haven't reached that level of recovery yet). Maybe, just like the spring, I will bloom in my own time.

Hating myself for my past never worked, but compassion did

The darkness is progressive; it gets worse. Being willing to see things differently is progressive, and the more you act upon it, the better it gets. The more I'm willing to see things differently, the more I realise that I wasn't a succubus that brought the downfall of everyone around her, or a damsel in distress who only had bad things done to her. I was somewhere in the middle.

I don't know you, but it's way more likely that you're an OK person who made some mistakes than a bad person. Somewhere in the swing between villainising and idealising ourselves, if we're aware that we've done things outside of our morals, it means we have them and can act on them now. We can be ashamed of what we did, but we can't be ashamed of who we are. We are a fallible human like everyone else, and our duty now is to do our best. Damning yourself as a monster, or indulging in lore that you're a sinister, Machiavellian antagonist when you're actually deep-fried in shame about your actions, doesn't leave room for growth. I thought facing myself meant I would just meet the reality that I was terrible, but really, I was just facing the fact that I have so many traits, like every human. Like every human, I can continue to act upon the change I want to make. People who grow self-awareness are very quick to recognise their shadow-side. Alongside that we can grow awareness around our more positive qualities, and be quicker to notice and act on those – like when we are intentionally kind, helpful and loving.

I have felt guilty, and drank the guilt away. The longer I stayed there, it turned into shame. I can't use my shame as a way to atone – that is only turning it into self-destruction, and self-hatred isn't an apology, nor does it benefit the people we have harmed. Shame doesn't go anywhere – it has no velocity; it only takes me down; it only burns inside and corrodes any chance of making anything right in the situation. While I try not to fixate on regret, no one is immune from that guilt-laden feeling over something they have or haven't done. I am the villain in some people's story, and I regret that. I will eternally endeavour to do what must be done to take responsibility for that and not repeat it. Inside the umbrella of regret we can find remorse, which involves self-appraisal and empathy, which can create a desire to make things right. With this empathy we acknowledge the feelings of the people involved, and it is from there that I do whatever I can to make it up to the people I have harmed so that we can all move on, which I will discuss in the next chapter.

In moving on with my past inside me, I must extend the empathy and compassion I feel naturally towards other people towards myself. Forgiving yourself isn't a luxury for the self-indulgent, it is a necessity for a life that is not wrestling the jaws of the shame of the past.

I don't hate the girl I was. It would be easy to put her in a box labelled 'bad Lauren' and hold her in contempt – but that is only rejecting a part of myself, one that already has an aggressive rejection wound. As I integrate myself into the world, I must integrate the past version of myself into my whole existence and give her acceptance. I draw her close, I pull her in and tell her she's safe now, because she survived so much to get here. She had the strength to learn lessons and change her behaviour when she easily could have petrified into a lifelong mission of resenting the world. The strength of my past self to go through that growing process is the very reason I am here. It would be judgemental and cruel to look down upon her now, when she did something so brave.

My behaviours had their purpose – in some ways they kept me alive when my options were 'kill yourself' or 'drink'. They saved me from the fear, abuse and confusion that felt too awful to face. They carried me through as the only tools I had. It was a contradiction, but it made sense. I was looking for something with their help. I made a deal with them to take these terrible things into their terrible care, and they worked, until they started taking everything else.

So many of the things we did that gave us shame-burn were done in moments when we literally had no other tools at our disposal. We were working with false intel, and we weren't capable with the limited skills we had of doing anything different. We have tools and skills now, and with self-forgiveness we become more aware of the good in us. Using our tools and skills, we can move ever closer to fully representing our true natures, the good in us and what we are capable of. It is when our behaviours line up with the internal sense of right and wrong that we uncover it becomes easier to live with yourself. We struggle less, and the more practice we get, the easier it is. The moments in the past become smaller as our life becomes bigger, and that space we create gives more examples of us living in line with our values.

I thought the way to get rid of my shame was by being perfect, when in reality it's acceptance

When you no longer surround yourself with, or participate in, shitty relationships, toxic work environments or one-way friendships you're met with the person who holds you to the highest standard of all – yourself. You can use other people's voices to tell you things you already feel about yourself. You become your own maniacal conductor, holding yourself to an imaginary standard of perfection. You are the demonic choreographer saying you aren't doing it right, your own shitty manager who was wondering angrily why you can't perform your duties to a suitable level. The most hateful things you believe about yourself can actually be calls coming from inside the house. This is a stark realisation, but a powerful one when you can acknowledge that you can let those narratives go, and live outside of them, gradually, in your daily actions.

You don't need to be universally adored to be accepted. You don't need your high-school bully to finally see how much they hurt you and track you down to apologise if you have the ability to accept yourself and share that with people who make you feel seen. You haven't failed at anything, because all the things that you thought might have made you perfect probably wouldn't have worked anyway. You only need as much time as necessary to mourn something that only existed in your imagination, and then find practical ways to find it in your reality today, in something more stable, secure and available to you.

When pain from the past claws at the wallpaper, letter writing is a safe way to get in contact with it. Rather than blocking it out or indulging it, with empathy for my past self I can put it into words. Writing is an action that can take you out of rumination, and it makes the things in your head something tangible. I usually find some clarity in the middle of a brain exorcism. When I am writing a letter to my past self, I include gratitude. There is also an apology, for all the self-harm and punishment. I make them as specific as possible, so that in my daily actions I am aware of all the ways I am growing. There is a corrective measure to every single harm I have done myself – for every unhealthy relationship I endured, it makes me commit further to seeking healthy ones today and not tolerating mistreatment. For every time I didn't speak up for myself when I didn't have the words, I will use my voice now even if it falters. For every friendship ruined, I protect the ones I have today. For every audition I blew, I now work on my craft, in whatever field I might be in today. For every scar on my body, I treat myself with conscious care.

Everything worth having in my life is something I could have lost, something I found along the way and something that isn't worth losing over temporary discomfort. You don't choose recovery for the bad days, but they come. It doesn't mean that it's all for nothing, and the past is waiting under a bridge to gobble you up. Recovery changes you, because you don't choose recovery to stay the same. If something didn't need to change, you wouldn't have made this decision, or have this decision become the only option.

And remember always: not everyone had a brain that tried to fucking kill them. You're probably doing a lot better than you think.

XIII. Repair and Restoration

> *Sobriety is less about "getting better" in a clear, linear sense than it is about subjecting yourself to change, to the inevitable ups and downs, fears and feelings, victories and failures, that accompany growth. You do get better — or at least you can — but that happens almost by default, by the simple fact of being present in your own life, of being aware and able, finally, to act on the connections you make.*
>
> – Caroline Knapp, *Drinking: A Love Story* (1996)

When going forward requires some going back and clearing some things out. When you've been doing the work, and things start to change. When you want to live comfortably with your darkness.

At just over a year sober I woke up with a weird space inside me. Something was missing. It wasn't a remarkable morning; it was the same grey splashes of a floral pattern on my sheets, the same jagged shadow of the window unit on the uneven floor of my room, the same heavy footsteps of a running group passing outside. But inside, the volume dial had been turned down, and in the quiet I had an intrinsic understanding that I was just another human, waking up to a day filled with cold sunshine. Not the worst, most pathetic person who had ever lived. I lay in bed a while and realised the thing that was missing was my desire to get off this planet. The space didn't exist as an aching void – it felt like possibility, curiosity and optimism. It wasn't just me and the dark thing I was trying to avoid any more. It was my first experience of peace of mind, which flickered and faded as the day started, but it was now something I knew was available to me. The space was created by the scaffolding I'd put up by committing to recovery, and it was being filled with a desire to start something new.

In my early days I was working against all the reasons not to keep going and feeling crunchy about the fact that I had to do these things (sorry, *get* to do these things). But from this point on, a year into my journey, despite the ups and downs, the list of reasons why I wanted to keep going got longer. I wanted to be a person who wrote cards for birthdays with words I meant, someone who was there for people whether or not I thought it could help, a safe and trusted person, who handled conflict well. My natural temperament to create things stirred. Now I'd tasted peace of mind, I didn't want to rob anyone of theirs. I wanted to be as reliable as I could be, and not treat any of my relationships as disposable or transactional.

As much as I wanted to say, 'You know, I could be on drugs right now and I'm not,' or, 'Sorry, I'm just really working on my recovery right now,' when someone wanted me to empty the dishwasher or do something boring, I wanted to have some sort of purpose, even if it was just being more helpful. I had shied away from responsibility in the past by saying I was unmanageable, stupid and disorganised. While I am capable of those traits, I was starting to realise I was capable of more. In areas where those traits were dominant (I can still perceive replying to an email as a personal Everest), I realised it didn't prohibit me from trying my absolute best, and seeing how it benefits everyone around me.

Acknowledging my struggle in areas of growth wasn't the same as getting stuck in it. The effort and continued attempts, alongside occasional successes, changed my beliefs about myself, outside shame – and before I could even notice it in myself people started to register that I was becoming more reliable. Someone even told me that she considered me one of her most practical friends. I argued with her and told her that I must have fooled her, or she was painfully oblivious. But the evidence was there. I was someone who was showing up, I was someone who turned up to the dentist on time and wasn't sending last-minute messages cancelling plans that had been in place for months. It was a fact I couldn't argue with, because it was the reality of my existence now.

At five years sober in 2023, after continuing to work on these things on a day-at-a-time basis, I felt something shift inside me again, a further integration of myself. Again, it wasn't a huge moment, I just woke up and drank a glass of water looking through the window at the view of East London, giving a wee wave to the people going to work on the Overground whizzing past my window, and people-watching the dog walkers and joggers along Regent's Canal. It sank in again: I was a part of this world, which had become so much more beautiful to me in the last five years. I was kind of just me, and I liked that person. Repairing my relationship with myself continued to repair my relationship with the world. One of the most important parts of that process was repairing my relationships with people, addressing things directly with those who'd been affected by my actions, if only to begin a demonstration of how I wanted to show up for them.

Nothing can touch me, neither praise nor disgrace, for I know what I am and, honestly, I was sometimes a dick. When I got sober, there were conversational topics with friends that were simply off-limits, from ruining someone's first DJ set by being taken away in an ambulance, to the charger incident of Christmas 2017 (we do not talk about the charger incident of Christmas 2017); things that festered (like how I prioritised my latest romantic obsession over being a reliable friend, colleague or employee) and tensions that sat on the edge of bubbling over into conflicts. Taking responsibility for my life has always been an empowering part of healing for me. Acknowledging the role you are playing in your suffering isn't blaming yourself, it's fighting your way out of a pattern. A part of that, for me, was taking responsibility for my actions in the past.***

I didn't really know how to make an honest apology, and yet I felt like I'd spent my whole life apologising for my entire existence. I wrote it, unprompted, in my sister's thirteenth birthday

---

*** Note: in a twelve-step fellowship, making direct amends to people you have harmed is step nine. If you are in a twelve-step fellowship or curious about one it is very important you do the previous eight steps before step nine, and do so with the direction of a sponsor.

card. I said it every time I came home because I knew I was going to fuck something up. I said, 'I'm sorry,' when I meant, 'I love you,' or, 'Please don't hate me.' I withdrew from people as an apology and took everything personally – it was sometimes easier to make something my fault than accept it was just unfair.

Things I don't need to apologise for:

Being raped.
Being a bit of an oddball sometimes.
Natural disasters.
Separating from people I have a harmful relationship with.
Something that has nothing to do with me.

Having a constantly apologetic mindset isn't the same as directly taking responsibility for what is yours. For me, that was simply an extension of shame, and made no space for change. My growth was apologising for my participation in harm caused to other people, and changing my behaviour. For people who over-apologise it's sometimes a healthy shift to say, 'Thank you for your patience,' rather than, 'Sorry for being late,' when something unavoidably disrupts travel plans, or, 'I'm grateful for your time,' rather than, 'Sorry I talk so much.' But a direct apology, with an intention to repair what might have been ruptured, is sometimes what other people need to feel recognised, and for us to externalise our intention going forward.

Things that aren't an apology:

Screaming, 'I'm fucking sorry, OK?' across the street.
Talking for ten minutes about what a piece of shit you are and how you don't deserve them.

Saying, 'I'm sorry I'm bitchy when you're being a dick.'
'I'm such a stupid fucking idiot, I can't believe I'm like this, for fuck's sake.'
'I'm sorry you feel that way,' when someone brings up something you absolutely did.
Creating a series of riddles for them to solve before you'll admit what you've done.
'You're wrong, but I'm sorry you're wrong.'

I am committed to change

My brother is a logical engineer who protects what he loves, has a sane and stable response to everything and displays flashes of laser-focused wit. My sister has an inspirational creativity that zones in on the exquisite side of everyday things; her intelligence and vision make the simple extraordinary. Even though we had our own rooms growing up, we would always sleep in each other's, simply because we loved being so close. They have never stopped loving me even when it would have been easy to. They have never stopped reminding me of who I was even when I forgot. I will never understand how I got so lucky.

I had texted my sister everything from, 'I am stuck in Russia and my visa has expired, don't tell Dad,' to, 'I'm in the psych ward again, but I promise I didn't try to kill myself.' She was just 16 years old, trying to study for her Highers and make sense of her own adolescence. I took up a lot of the airtime in the family growing up, because my issues overrode any my brother and sister were having. I didn't need to apologise for being mentally ill, but I could apologise for the actions that I regretted: overloading them with my issues when they, too, were children;

disappearing on them when they needed me and the spiteful comments I made out of envy that they seemed to be so well adjusted when I was struggling with the role of eldest daughter. Talking to my parents, I had to recognise that for a long time they were as happy as their least happy child. For the longest time that was me, and I took it out on them. I could acknowledge how much it must have hurt to have your first child be so lost, distant and angry, that they were great parents and that I wanted to be close to them now. It wasn't a shame-based exercise, because I can't shame myself for being a child acting like a child. It was a recognition of the past and what I could have done better, and the changes I would make to strive to do so now, so we could get out of it.

I gave them the opportunity to speak, and this jagged edge that ran through our childhood became a series of things that happened, rather than a tripwire we were always trying to step around. The transparency meant that if I go to that place again, we have more information. None of us were required to be perfect, simply open and truthful without being condemning.

All they asked for, when I invited them to share anything they wanted to, was my participation as a daughter and sister. I started calling more, simply to ask how their day was going and listening to the answer (my parents know the name and interpersonal dynamics of every single one of their cows; there's a lot of ground to cover). I committed to participating in buying Christmas presents, organising meet-ups and taking on responsibility rather than saying, 'That's not my burden to bear, I'm the family liability.' Eventually it grew, and I found myself doing the right thing under the worst circumstances, like when my mum went to hospital and I was able to get there as soon as I could and help keep the house running as she recovered. I brought a lot of pain into my family, and now I get to bring recovery into my family. Not as an evangelical or from a place of superiority – simply as a member. Even if you feel like the black sheep of the family, you don't have to dye yourself to fit in, you can simply bring all the unique qualities that black sheep have.

Sometimes when I was with my friends I felt like I was in a state of retroactive humiliation. Some of the events were still jokes, examples of our reckless youth, but the more my friends were reflecting on the past, the more we started to think about these things in different ways. My friend and musical collaborator Fionnuala had the honour of taking me to A&E twice. This apology started with heartfelt thanks that she took care of me at my most vulnerable (and for always bringing a pair of tights that didn't have holes in them and deodorant to our recitals), and an apology for all the times I didn't recognise the toll it took on her. My friend Philip, who lay sleepless next to me in case I choked on my own vomit, thanked me for my honesty, and affirmed to me that we were in this together, but if I ever made us wander the streets of Glasgow in December all night again, because I checked my coat with our keys and phones in it, got kicked out of the club for falling down the stairs, lost the cloakroom ticket, then lost all chance of retrieving them because I had a fight with a bouncer, we would have a problem. Some people told me a lot of things that were hard to listen to, but we breathed a sigh of relief when we let it go.

Having a vulnerable conversation and being able to survive it is healthy for strengthening friendships. It allowed me to stay committed to doing things in a way that meant we didn't have to worry about each other, and had clarity to make the boundaries that sustain us. It was gradual work, where my words and actions had to meet each other.

A lot of people made it very clear that they never wanted to hear from me again, and that inserting myself back into their lives for the sake of making an apology wouldn't be appropriate, because I can't betray people's boundaries just to make myself feel better. Sometimes you have to make peace with the fact that not everyone will forgive you even when you're genuinely sorry, and you need to be able to forgive yourself and still move on. If they don't want to hear from me, they won't hear from me. A way I make it up to my exes is not to text my exes. I still had a cautious connection with Kweku, even though I completely convinced him during the break-up that he had destroyed me and I would never be the same again. I was able to tell him he was a good man, and a great boyfriend, who took space when he should have. It let us both move on, and not carry amputated limbs of our past relationships into our new ones. What's mine is mine and what's theirs is theirs, and the weight of what happened in the past isn't ours to carry any more; we can start putting it down.

I didn't approach people who I had an abuse dynamic with, even though I sometimes wanted to in a perverse way, because it would give me a sense of control over a narrative. Sometimes you feel bad because you need to apologise, sometimes something bad happened, and you offer yourself closure by telling yourself it's closed and healing what needs to be healed inside yourself. I do not offer two-way communication to receive people's contempt as I am an equal member in all my relationships today.

The strangest part of directly and honestly addressing my past was seeing how many people had forgiven me. It made me consider what I was willing to let go of, like hating people who didn't help me, when I was in no position to be helped and everyone else, just like me, was working with the tools they had at the time. I thought forgiveness was an act of signing the deed of how I did something wrong and they were right all along, and in this exercise I was able to find what forgiveness meant to me – that I was willing to let go of the anger for greater clarity.

Have I forgiven my childhood abuser, the people who have assaulted me and people in positions of power doing their worst? Sometimes the anger I'm holding onto about those situations reminds me that it shouldn't have happened, and I deserved better, and sometimes I can affirm that without the anger. Sometimes I can fully understand that some people hurt me when they were as clueless and boundaryless as I was, and forgive by chalking it all up to growing up. Sometimes I resent the work it's taken and sometimes it doesn't touch me. Forgiveness, like healing, isn't always linear, and some days I'm indignant at the treatment I've received, and some days I'm genuinely wishing everyone well. This may be a stage, or it might be what forgiveness looks like for me in this lifetime, but I'm willing to keep experimenting with it.

When forgiveness was introduced to me as a concept I thought I was being duped into forgiving my abuser, but rather than fly off into an extreme or universal imperative, I could simply consider whether I could enhance my life by being less hard on the people I loved by hanging onto things. I could ask myself, 'Would it serve or hurt me more to let go of a grievance or to keep thinking hatefully upon that person? Would it make a conflict easier or harder to negotiate if I consider that the intentions are good based on the evidence I have, or assign malice to them based on something I can't let go of? Is icing someone out for my self-protection, or am I just not willing to have a hard conversation or move on from something that is only being kept alive by living it over and over in my head?'

Forgiveness does not mean that you are excusing or co-signing bad behaviour. It is letting go of the power something holds over you, and accepting that people are who they are and that what happened happened. It is cutting a cord to the past, releasing a force held over you, and transmuting it into something that can move forwards, whatever that might be.

But what if I do my best and I fuck up anyway?

Being in recovery doesn't make me exempt from making mistakes. I will continue to fuck up. I will be short with people for taking the bins out wrong, be the tutting and sighing commuter I never wanted to become when people start walking into the Tube without letting people off and I will forget birthdays and anniversaries. I will make bad decisions. When my move to London turned into an unmitigated disaster I called my friend Christian to moan about how I'd done all this work and still made such a stupid decision.

He said to me: 'When did you think you'd start making perfect decisions?'

There is no life exempt from mistakes. Recovery doesn't happen when everything is going well, it happens when you fuck up and do something different in the aftermath. You may even find that what seems like a bad decision might not have been a mistake, it might have been what needed to happen. Recovery happens in the missteps and fuck-ups we work our way back from, when we don't know if everything is going to be OK, but we keep going regardless.

There's a parallel universe running somewhere, in which I didn't have the moment of grace when I realised help was available and decided that I wanted to do the things to get and, hopefully, stay sober. There's a timeline where things keep getting worse. However, I don't believe in 'before and after'. I don't believe I was 'bad' then and 'good' now, even though I do significantly fewer shitty things now, and know how to make a meaningful apology. I don't think the gifts of sobriety are little treats or rewards from the universe for being a good girl or doing something inherently pure, or because I've been specially chosen. They are the consequences of working hard, living with a bit more integrity, learning to accept myself and being open to receiving grace. At the same time, the awful things that happen outside of my control aren't punishments. Life has a life of its own, where things are unfair. You get ghosted and you try to tell yourself it's because they just loved you too much to text you back when in reality you liked them more than they liked you. Your parents get sick and you realise that they've aged the same fifteen years you have but they have less time left. The wrong person dies and you have to live with it. I can work on myself as hard as I like, I can engage with my sobriety as much as I can, and those things will still happen, and they will still hurt. One of the most important things I have ever been told is that because life has a life of its own, my sobriety must have a life of its own, where I choose it even when it feels like it isn't working.

There are no perfect decisions or perfect recovery, because aside from being sober I am human. I struggle. I wish I could say my sobriety date was the last time I purged but it wasn't – it was the day Dominic and I realised over a silent dinner table that we had stopped loving each other. I wish the last time I thought about suicide was my sobriety date, but it wasn't – it was when I realised that I had all the potential to become a successful opera singer, my dreams became available to me and I didn't want them. I wish the last time I cheated, shouted, fought and lied was my sobriety date, but I've done all those things in sobriety and faced the consequences. I can go non-verbal. I repeat the same sentence over and over in distress. I have felt trapped by sobriety when I would rather just lose my shit. I have pages and pencils on my desk to tear and snap. I had to buy a new cafetière this week because I threw it in the sink when I couldn't believe how stupid I was not to clean it out the night before. I sometimes give strangers the best of me and lash out at the people who love me. Sometimes when I'm sad I worry if it's depression coming back to take me for good this time, and I miss the split second when a substance hits your system and everything feels magical – the part before it becomes not enough. I wish the last time I thought about drinking was before that day when I realised for the first time that I wanted to be part of the human race, but it wasn't. It was the day I was told I was going to get the chance to write a book about sobriety, and I got very frightened that it wouldn't be good enough.

I've also had more joy in sobriety than I can measure in any metric. I always feel like I have to add that, especially talking about the harder things. It's important, because we must remember it's worth it, but there's a sort of style I fall into where I prise open the pain and try to balance it with some sort of conclusive message. Wholeness isn't turning every negative into a positive – it doesn't always need to be packaged as a neat, tidy and digestible lesson. Part of the grief is accepting that things have happened that have left me forever altered. It can be painful, but it isn't a tragedy. I will still continue in the most restorative way I know how. These truths exist in the same place – that's just being alive.

The dark streak

There are many ways people describe their darkness: the shitty friend, the shadowy companion, that thing they can't ignore. Some people say it's the ditch beside them, the reminder of what they can fall into if they don't keep growing. People see it as a black hole that shrinks the more they fill their life with light. Some people feel it as a fog that takes them over if they're not watching.

I feel mine like a current. It's the surging riptide of my mean streak when I feel threatened, it's my overwhelming tendency to want to escape, it's the zap in my brain that says, 'You know what would fix this? A big fat drink.' It's the echoing thud in my head that says, 'No one would care if you died,' and my only comfort is imagining people being very sad at my funeral. It's something I can fall into and it will take me. It grows if I feed it, and can be a soft buzz or a killer shock, depending on how I'm protecting myself.

I have resolved to share my darkness, because I do not believe that salvation is granted only to people who manage to fully and wholly oust this thing inside them, and that they are the only ones worth listening to. I didn't feel comforted by people who had achieved perfect healing, I was comforted by people who said, 'I feel that, too.' I didn't get sober to cut parts of myself off, I got sober to integrate all the parts of myself in a way that doesn't hurt any more, only leaving behind the parts that no longer fit or have stopped working.

We need everyone at the table. People who have managed to harness the darkness, people who don't have the same brand of darkness, people who are submerged in it, people who are hungover but willing to start again, people who are angrily texting anyone who will listen about how bullshit sobriety is, people who are decades away from a drink, people who are three minutes away from their first one in a while whether they want it or not.

Pillars

It's a weird contradiction to have a brain that tried to convince you that you were better off dead, and sometimes still can. Repair and restoration can be messy, tough and demoralising at times. If you have a dark streak, or sit with the complex title of 'survivor', your recovery changes from scaffolding to a row of pillars that holds the structure of your life together, and you can keep building new ones as you go – playful, pleasurable and hopeful things to encourage you and help you grow when you need to keep on going. When you live with a dark streak, there has to be something running alongside it. Something just as powerful. Even if we're struggling, we're learning how to struggle better.

Some pillars I polish today

Play

Out of necessity, recovery involves structure, discipline and doing the opposite of the more tempting dramatic release. For our recovery and our humanity, we can find places in our life where we can achieve a state of play.

For many of us the idea of play was abandoned after childhood; it doesn't have a space in our adult lives. Women are raised to be nurturers, or girlbosses, or both, and whichever you choose, you're wrong, selfish, vain or settling. Losing myself in something, being silly or really enjoying something when I could be either rearing children or building a career, felt wrong. Having it take up so much of the airtime in my brain seemed to serve no purpose.

Play has always been necessary, though. It's where children learn skills for later life, like how to get along with others, planning, organisation, emotional regulation and how to cope with stress. Some of us who had life drag them up a bit more quickly than anticipated might not have even had a playful childhood, so it has even less of a presence in adulthood. As adults, any craft or hobby we pick up feels like it should be monetised to make it worth something, which stops it from being play and it becomes another thing we have to do excellently to prove our worth.

It might seem condescending to call adult activities like watching sports, making music or getting into nature as play – it feels vulnerable to do something coded as childish as a part of our adult life – but it is a necessary part of being alive. Play is progressive: the more playful you are, the more play you attract.

There are things in life you must take seriously, but if your world gets small and serious, you can wonder why you even bother being a survivor. You don't need to aim for joy, but you can aim for play and see what happens. Usually, you get a bit joyful.

Pleasure

Feeling pleasure after feeling nothing is something necessary for survival. You fought hard for this body, and after it felt every type of hurt, you are allowed some pleasure.

When you're a pleasure seeker who fell down the abyss, pleasure can be frightening – you can wonder whether it's just the beginning of a new fixation to eject you from the experience of being alive. But when you're viewing pleasure as something you get as a result of actions you take in your life, rather than something you are trying to inject into your life to make it bearable, it can feel like enough. You can experience the pleasure of going slowly, making a decision, being present in a way that doesn't hurt. So many pleasures in the past came hard and fast: the hit of a drug, feeling held by a drink, the sensation of someone sliding into you when you aren't sure if you want that, or a hug and a cup of tea. There is a pleasure in the certainty that you are choosing what you want, and accessing the experience in a way that ensures you are not afraid of the comedown.

The difference between a superficial hit and pleasure is presence. If you have presence in your pleasure, rather than manically sucking the life out of it, it turns into contentment, or even joy – two things that don't require more. It has enough, and enough is a feast. No one can sell it to you, and you can't be manipulated into it.

Hope

When you're a survivor, your existence gives people hope, and having experienced hopelessness, we know how important the smallest indication of hope can be. One of the most hopeful things we can do is help one another. Even if it goes unrecognised, we can support the hopeful future that something good might come of this.

Helping, and loving, others is literally the only thing in life that matters outside of the meeting of our basic needs. It isn't something I undertake as a course or a weekend venture to get away from myself. I try to make it the foundation of my existence, both in my work and the time I spend in the world as a human being who knows she is more than her job. The human being who spends time with friends, interacts with strangers, has fun and is a member of families, communities and neighbourhoods.

This is what gives me hope. That we're all in this together, surviving it all, and choosing to love and understand each other even when it's hard.

Conclusion

Clearing out a drawer yesterday, I found a small stack of casino membership cards, all bearing a different variation of my surname (I do not know who Lauren McQuistib is, but I know she wasn't sober). Casinos were one of my liminal spaces of choice when I got kicked out of clubs or had nowhere else to go, spaces with oxygen pumping through the artificial daytime, machines pinging and clicking with the anticipation of 'this one is going to be the one', and watered-down vodka. I never gambled there, I just sat quietly by myself, running the conversations I'd have with people the next day about how much fun I'd had last night. I would wonder if anyone would take me out of here, if 'the one' was in a casino at 5 a.m. I would sit down inside myself, in this place where time didn't exist, and wish there wasn't another world out there that I had to return to.

One of the best things about leaving the casino, sitting down inside yourself and finding out who you really are is realising you can do whatever you want with your life. One of the scariest things about leaving the casino, sitting down inside yourself and finding out who you really are is realising you can do whatever you want with your life – and no one else can do it for you.

It's harder than pulling a lever, but it can still feel like a huge gamble, and like the world outside is the malevolent house that will always win.

I am not in here with a pre-ordained destiny to come out with less than I came in with. I'm here to direct my attention, change my ideas the more I learn, and feel it all. I can make choices now, rather than just winding up in the same place and wondering how I got there. Sometimes they aren't good choices – sometimes they are even bad ones – but they're mine. There is a good deal of it that is still up to fate and luck, but the stakes are different. My commitment is to leave the world better than I found it, even in a small way, and if I am giving in that way, I lose nothing.

Growing up, we had a chest of drawers called the 'comfy drawers' because we didn't know where all the stuff inside 'comes fae'. Recovery is taking a look inside the drawers and just dealing with what's inside. Going through what seems like an indiscriminate mess, realising what is ours, what is something we picked up along the way, what is something that used to serve us and now doesn't, things we lost and things we have been looking for but didn't know we still had. There's usually a tangle of cables, too, which gets in the way and has to be unravelled.

You don't unravel simply to fall apart; you unravel to fit together better, so you can have a comfortable experience of just being yourself. I found out that I like being around people. I'm not extroverted, I just wanted attention, and yet I'm not as introverted as I thought; I was just scared of being myself around people. I love making music with strangers but not in the way I thought; I prefer San Pellegrino to Highland Spring, but honestly I once smashed a bottle of vodka on the floor at Girvan station and had to be convinced not to drink it off the ground so tap is fine; I love staying in – oh, I really love staying in – but it turns out I really love dancing; I make a really good roast; I can be in pubs and not drink; love is everything to me; I really should take magnesium – it does help; being able to help someone gives me everything I thought being famous would; Nicholas is still my best friend and I pray that everyone gets to experience a love like that; I actually can meditate, and I want to live. When I got drunk for the first time and kissed that boy at the Battle of the Bands, I thought, *There is no greater feeling on Earth than this.* I chased the idea of feeling that feeling again until I almost died. I'm six years sober now, and can honestly say that there is no greater feeling on Earth than waking up sober.

You can keep watering dead plants, or you can start a new garden. You can keep being frustrated at how stuck you are, or you can change the soil. You can cut and run or persist. You can be unsure which path to take and wait for a new one, or create one out of nothing – that's what getting into recovery is some of the time.

Not drinking is just the beginning

I am willing to take an honest look at how I am participating in my suffering, but not to pick up any sticks to beat myself with. Soon, the non-drinking becomes the easy part, and the hard part is maintaining a life you care about. It's strange when you find the life outside of 'working with the tools I had at the time'. There's a strange moment when something that was lost doesn't return, and you don't mind so much, when you sit inside your body and it just is. There's an odd intrusiveness when the voice in your head stops telling you you're pathetic, and it's replaced with thinking of someone's anniversary, wondering if you took your vitamins that morning of if you should call your mum. Sobriety isn't just a choice you make, it's a thing you practise daily, for the pursuit of wholeness, to live truthfully, joyfully and helpfully. But I still have to commit to choosing it every day.

When you've tried to kill yourself, you have a weird relationship with being alive. It gives me this strange sense of time and the moment I'm inhabiting, because it all seems so surreal that I get to live like this. I can get nostalgic for the exact moment I'm in, because I now know how growth works, and every second I am in will one day be long ago. I know that I'm made up of tiny decisions, second chances and taken opportunities, and, being a naturally reflective person, I treat them with significance, I treasure them. I'm allowed to – this was all so unlikely.

Thank you for listening to my story

People's stories gave me the courage to get sober, especially the ones that didn't hide from the darkness or follow neat patterns – the ones that gripped me and steered me into willingness were the ones that acknowledged that there is chaos, there is pain, there is darkness – but despite that you can still do something good. I didn't get sober because people were perfect, I got sober because people were honest. Standing honestly in our own experience is one of the touchstones of becoming whole, and people's courageous examples made me believe it was possible for me, too; that I could not only understand myself, but experience myself. Experiencing yourself isn't a performance, and when you truly do this, you create ripples. When you stand in your recovery it doesn't just benefit you. The internal change impacts the people and places you encounter with the loving actions you take. It was never just about us. Recovery is for everyone.

It isn't delusional to believe you are capable, resourceful and skilled in the spaces where you exist. It's actually vital that you believe this, so you can act on it. When you do this, the evidence grows, and you can really start believing it. There's flexibility in this space to learn more, and also change your ideas about yourself. This is absolutely necessary when you've spent a lot of time hating yourself and fixating on what you believe you lack.

If there is one thing I want you to take from this book it's that you are a vital human, and no matter how mundane or unremarkable you think your story is, it might save someone. You are necessary. You do something only you can do for someone, as you, at this moment in time. You deserve dignity and respect, because you are sacred.

When people told me their stories of how it got better, I had been in so much pain for so long I couldn't even conceive of a better life, so I didn't know what better meant. I was told not to quit before the miracle happened, but I didn't even know what a miracle was. I couldn't even appreciate the one in my own front yard (the fact that I was alive). How could I have even known what a life beyond my wildest dreams was, when I hadn't even had dreams before – only delusions and demands. I couldn't think my way through it; I had to show up every day and find out.

I hope this is just the beginning. I began my day today with a quiet cup of coffee, lying on my stomach, in bed with my arms propping me up. I haven't washed my hair, and I'm wearing a jumper three sizes too big, with bare legs. There's a hand on my back and the sheets are twisted from crawling back into them at 8.45 a.m. I have one of the busiest weeks I've had in a while coming up, there are rail strikes and my body is changing since I stopped punishing it, but I've taken this hour today not to complain about any of it and enjoy this cup of coffee in bed.

When he handed me the coffee I said thank you because I'm polite now, and I am overwhelmed by the fact that he only has a dimple on one side of his face and I never knew I could love a dimple so much. And it's then I realise that I'm living the life I thought I could never have, the one I prayed for, for so long. I wanted to be sober long before I admitted it to myself, and I woke up sober this morning, with an intention to stay that way today. When I thought about a sober life before I didn't factor in happiness; I thought that was a bridge too far and I wasn't going to get ahead of myself. I wasn't to know what was about to happen, and that's probably for the best because if you'd told me, I wouldn't have believed you. I would keep myself up at night as a child worrying about the meaning of life, and I tentatively settled on the idea that I could only hope to do good and have it mean something, so it looks like her prayer was answered, too. I used to beg something I didn't believe in yet to help me stop injuring myself on purpose because I needed something bad to happen to match my insides, and now I'm a bit more aware that my scars have been healed over for almost six years now. And my hungry heart knows that I can have coffee in bed on a Wednesday morning with someone, without worrying when they're going to find out who I really am and hate me for it. Most of all, there's nothing to fear today, even if the worst happens.

He says it looks like I'm really enjoying my coffee, and I say, 'Yeah, I really am.'

We don't have to have it all worked out yet, we just have to see what we can do today. We don't need to know where it is taking us, we just need to keep showing up as best we can. Very simply, I have regretted drinking, but I have never regretted getting sober. We are exactly where we need to be. We're at the beginning.

Acknowledgements

I am endlessly grateful to The Society of Authors and the Authors' Foundation grant, which allowed me to write this book - thank you for your support and the work you do.

Like my recovery, this book has only been possible because I have been helped and supported by people who are much wiser than I am. Thank you to Marleigh, for replying to my 'I-want-to-write-a-book,-how-do-I-do-that' text, and helping me start this whole process, to my agent, Daisy Chandley, for guiding me, believing wholeheartedly in this project and saving my sanity regularly, to my editors Danielle Pender and Michelle Kane, for their skill, patience and guidance, to Lola Downes and Vikki Warner for their insight, and to the whole team at 4th Estate and Blackstone Publishing.

Thank you to Cat Marnell, who inspired and encouraged me from the beginning, to Alex, Grace (my tippy tap gals), Fran, Vic, David and Sophie, for reading chapters in various drafts and giving incredible, valuable feedback, to Josh, Giovanni, Charlotte and Max for getting me out of my head when I was stuck, and always making me laugh, and to my subscribers on Patreon, who read and supported my writing before anyone else even knew about it.

Thank you to all the people who contributed their experience to the book, to the hundreds of people who have impacted my recovery with their commitment to their own and the spirit of helpfulness, to the sober women who keep me grateful, to Christian, Katya, Sarah, Fiona and Emily for helping me more than they'll ever know and to everyone at the Keddlestone Community Centre.

Thank you to my best friend, Nicholas, for absolutely everything, and to Mum, Dad, Gavin and Caroline, for their unwavering support.

Finally, thank you to Chris Chung, the Mancunian bowling doctor, for being my stable base, offering daily love and encouragement and for listening to me read out every version of each chapter without judging or loving me any less because of its content.

Endnotes

Introduction
1. Drinkaware (2022). *Alcohol Consumption UK.* [online] Drinkaware.co.uk. Available at: https://www.drinkaware.co.uk/research/alcohol-facts-and-data/alcohol-consumption-uk
2. ScienceDaily (n.d.). *More young adults are abstaining from alcohol.* [online] Available at: https://www.sciencedaily.com/releases/2020/10/201012120007.htm
3. Cigna (2022). *Exhausted by Work – The Employer Opportunity.* [online] Cigna. Available at: https://www.cigna.com.hk/iwov-resources/docs/Cigna-360-Global-Well-being-Survey.PDF
4. www.gov.scot. (n.d.). 2. *Alcohol and Drug Use Prevalence and Harms: Latest Data and Trends.* [online] Available at: https://www.gov.scot/publications/review-existing-literature-evidence-young-people-experiencing-harms-alcohol-drugs-scotland/pages/3/
5. AlphaBiolabs (2022). *Drug use among young people up 75% since 2021*, charity finds | AlphaBiolabs UK. [online] Available at: https://www.alphabiolabs.co.uk/blog/

drug-use-among-young-people-up-75-since-2021-charity-finds/

II. Fear
1. Forward Trust (2024). *Challenging the stigma surrounding drugs, alcohol and other addictions at your workplace – Forward Trust.* [online] Available at: https://www.forwardtrust.org.uk/support-us/company-support/challenging-the-stigma-surrounding-drugs-alcohol-and-other-addictions-at-your-workplace/ [Accessed 4 Dec. 2024]
2. Carl Erik Fisher (2022). *The Urge: Our History of Addiction.* Penguin. 258.
3. The Global Commission on Drug Policy (2017). *The War on Drugs.* [online] Available at: https://www.globalcommissionondrugs.org/reports/the-war-on-drugs
4. Carl Erik Fisher (2022). *The Urge: Our History of Addiction.* Penguin. 150.
5. Ahmad, D. L. (2000). *Opium smoking, anti-Chinese attitudes, and the American medical community, 1850–1890.* American Nineteenth Century History, 1(2), pp.53–68. doi:https://doi.org/10.1080/14664650008567016

VI. Escapism
1. NICE (2020). *Self-harm: How common is it?* [online] NICE. Available at: https://cks.nice.org.uk/topics/self-harm/background-information/prevalence/

VIII. The Internet
1. Dennis, A. B. (2024). *Eating Disorder Risk Factors –* National Eating Disorders Association. [online] National

Eating Disorders Association. Available at: https://www.nationaleatingdisorders.org/risk-factors/

2. Teen Help (2015). *Teen Eating Disorder Statistics.* [online] Available at: https://www.teenhelp.com/eating-disorders/teen-eating-disorder-statistics/

3. Mental Health Foundation (2022). *Loneliness in young people: research briefing.* [online] www.mentalhealth.org.uk. Available at: https://www.mentalhealth.org.uk/our-work/public-engagement/unlock-loneliness/loneliness-young-people-research-briefing